A Common Man
Ikce Wicasa

Modern Lakota Spirituality
and Practice
Words and Wisdom from
Sidney Keith
and
Melvin Miner

by Kevin Thomas

Copyright © 2013 Kevin Thomas
dragonfly press
contact us at acommonman2012-book@yahoo.com

This book was previously issued as an eBook. Changes have been made in punctuation and content added for clarification.

Edited by Estella Ella Claymore
Cover photo by Kevin Thomas
Cover design by Seth Thomas
All rights reserved

This book may not be reproduced in whole or in part without written permission from the publisher, except by a reviewer who may quote brief passages in a review; nor may any part of this book be reproduced, stored in a retrieval system, or transmitted in any form or by any means electronic, mechanical, photocopying, recording, or other, without written permission from the publisher

ISBN-13: 978-0615836003
ISBN-10: 0615836003

Eagle Butte News 1975

Visitors and dancers from all over the United States are expected for the fourth annual Sun Dance and Calf Pipe Ceremony which will be held this weekend, August 15-17 at Green Grass. This year's Sun Dance Ceremonial will be dedicated to the Great Mystery Wankantanka. "Prayers with the Sacred Calf-Pipe Bundle will include the great vision we are about to see so that all brothers and sisters will not suffer long," said Sioux Nation Arts Council President Sidney Keith. "Sun Dancers are urged to fast before they can participate. The weather will be hot and dry and will be right for the Sun Dancing and we trust that we will see a vision. Many visions have been seen at Green Grass for the past three years for directions for all Native

Americans to follow," said Keith. There are good camping grounds and water. Two meals a day will be provided to all Native Americans. A Pow Wow will be held nightly under a separate bowery. Alcohol will not be permitted on the ceremonial grounds and tight security will be enforced.

A note on the text. Most of the dialogue and text found in this book is written word for word from the people who said them. Their words can include improper use of grammar and misspelled words. Please note that these mistakes were intentionally left in to give the reader a sense of who these men were, in order to hear their voice through the pages.

for peggy

Acknowledgements

Any project of this nature is a group undertaking. I have received help from a great number of people from start to finish while creating this book. I wish to thank the family of Melvin Miner II - Jodee, Melvin III, Calvin, and Melorie. I wish to thank Merle Whistler for his infinite patience. I thank Estella Ella Claymore from the bottom of my heart for her professional editing. Thank you to the family of Sidney Keith, especially Sandy. In no particular order I wish to thank Mark Claymore, Marlyce Miner, Inyan Hoksila and all Sun Dancers everywhere. Also to Ian Frazier, Thomas E. Mails, Vic Glover, Peter Matthiessen, Mark St. Pierre and Tilda Long Soldier for the inspiration to keep on going. Many thanks to the friendly people of South Dakota for their hospitality. Last but not the least to my family for putting up with my long absences while I traveled and wrote this book. To anyone I may have forgotten, I humbly thank as well. I also thank the Creator for all the gifts given.
Wopila Tunkashila

Contents

Prologue - 1

1: Sidney Keith – Origins 6

2: Melvin Miner –
A Ceremony for his Mother 15

3: Sidney Keith -
Origin of the Sun Dance 22

4: Melvin Miner –
College Days 29

5: Sidney Keith –
Spirits at the Creation 42

6: Melvin Miner –
Melvin Leaves College 49

7: Sidney Keith –
Origin of the Pipestone 63

8: Melvin Miner –
A Pow Wow for Rapid City 68

9: Sidney Keith –
Sun Dance Story 75

10: Melvin Miner –
Melvin's First Sun Dance 81

11: Sidney Keith –
Stones and Spirits 112

12: Melvin Miner -
The Mark on the Forehead 122

13: Sidney Keith –
Family History of Medicine People 134

14: Melvin Miner –
A Trip to New York City 144

15: Sidney Keith – Heyoka- 160

16: Sidney Keith - Black Magic 173
17: Melvin Miner –
Indian Land for Sale 180
18: Melvin Miner –
Curing a Spiritual Leader 186
19: Sidney Keith –
Martin High Bears Vision 195
20: Melvin Miner –
Dogs - 203
21: Melvin Miner –
Indian Names 210
22: Melvin Miner –
Treaties 216
23: Melvin Miner –
Sidney Keith Stories 225
24: Melvin Miner –
Holding the Sacred Pipe 233
25: Melvin Miner - Pipe Protocol 264
26: Melvin Miner - The Four Ages 277
27: Melvin Miner - Sidney Keith –
Food 285
28: Sidney Keith – Assimilation 290
29: Sidney Keith - Mitakuye Oyasin 300
Epilogue 303
Chapter Notes 305
Glossary 314

Prologue

In late July of 2009, I was in Eagle Butte, South Dakota, to attend my first Sun Dance. I was invited by Melvin "Mel" Miner Jr. whom I had been friends with for about four years at that time. We were driving around town while he showed me different places of interest from his childhood. His grandfather had been the jailer for the county jail for many years, in fact the new county jail was named for him. Melvin took me by the old jail where his grandparents had lived. In the back of the property, there was a radio tower that Mel had started to climb one day as a child. He told me that he froze from being afraid of the height and then had to be rescued. Mel laughed as he talked about how far off the ground it had seemed at the time.

As the day progressed, we went into several stores in town where Melvin sold some of his crafts; several times he stopped and talked to old friends and relatives. We went by the Cheyenne River Sioux Tribal office so he could get a new tribal identification card. The secretary looked at me and asked if I needed one too. I almost said yes. At some point we stopped at the H. V. Johnson Cultural Center located on the main highway through town. Several times Mel had pointed out that his father-in-law had lived and worked in Eagle Butte and had raised a family there. At the cultural center, we went into a big multiuse room which was decorated with several giant sized murals.

"My father-in-law Sidney Keith painted these murals," Melvin said. "He was an artist and he also had a sign painting business. He worked for the Indian hospital for years. He was also the Medicine Man I learned the most from."

What a well-rounded life I thought to myself. Melvin was explaining what was depicted in several of the paintings.

"That painting is the inside of the Sweat Lodge. It's pitch dark inside, but the Medicine Man can see in the dark somehow. You or I can't see anything in there, but the Medicine Man can."

"I've never been in a Sweat Lodge before," I said.

Melvin shook his head.

"We'll have to take care of that before the Sun Dance. You have to purify yourself before the ceremony starts," Melvin said.

A sense of dread came over me, remembering a bad experience with a sauna years before. "Well how hot does it get in there?" I asked.

"Not too hot. For you beginners, we'll only let your flesh blister so much before we drag you out." Then he laughed and looked at me, gauging my reaction.

I had known Melvin for a few years but hadn't spent very much time with him. I was quickly learning to appreciate his wicked sense of humor though. He and I spent hours that day talking about growing up in the 1970's, the cars we used to have, concerts we had seen and the parties we went to. He was about six years older than me and reminded me of some of my older cousins I had when I was growing up.

At some point during the day Mel said, "You know, my father-in-law started the International Sun Dance in Green Grass. It was the first Sun Dance in modern times on the Cheyenne River Indian Reservation. They had to practice their religion underground 'til then because it was illegal. So he got Fools Crow and some other people and started the Sun Dance, and later on he was a Medicine Man. He helped a lot of people. He worked to keep the language alive too. He wrote his own dictionary. You know, someone with some time on their hands, and the ability could write a book about him."

So, the seed was planted.

I lived in Illinois and Melvin lived in Rapid City, South Dakota. Given the distance involved we decided to use an old fashioned tape recorder to start taking notes. The plan was for Melvin to put his thoughts on the tape and then mail the tape to me. We got started in earnest that November. One day a box of tapes arrived in the mail. I called Melvin and told him the package had arrived. I spent about a month transcribing the tapes and putting them on the computer. I wound up sending him packages of notes in the mail, the old fashioned way.

I traveled to South Dakota several times that next year, staying at Melvin's place and also traveling back to Eagle Butte for the Sun Dance. Several times when I arrived in Rapid City late at night we would sit and talk until nearly daybreak. We didn't just talk about the book but about everything. We both had adult children and we marveled at how it seemed that parenthood was payback time. He also had some great "shaggy dog" stories that unfortunately won't make it into this book. What did make it into this book was the result of many hours of those conversations, phone calls and research.

One - Sidney Keith
Origins

I was born eight miles west of the Moreau River in Bear Creek, South Dakota. In my family there were only two boys, I'm the oldest. My dad died when I was 14-years-old. Most of the time growing up I spent with my grandmother and grandfather. I liked them so well that's who I spent most of my time with. I followed my grandfather around because he liked to tell stories. He talked with the older men about their hunts and they told each other how they used to do this hunting, riding, and chasing buffalo. So I learned all those things; all about the culture and all the ways to survive when in a big storm and what to do in case of an emergency and all that stuff. He'd even tell me these stories at noon. He always talks with the older people and that's where I learned to listen to the stories and I learned quite a bit. Some of these are some of the older men, he grew up with them. They sit around and talk about their hunt and I used to sit there and just listen hour after hour. When my mother came out to look for me, I'd always be there. I'd be laying on my belly or laying on my back or sitting up and I used to listen to my grandfather.

My grandmother, at night she'd tell *wocahie* (animal) stories, that were easy to tell. She would keep talking till one of us goes to sleep, she keeps talking till I go to sleep, and she never finished telling the story. Every day, every month, every year till my parents they were there, she'd teach us three or four different stories. She would tell us *iktomi* (spider) stories about a giant *iktomi*. That's what I learned from my grandmother.

In later years, my grandfather was a Medicine Man. He used to have to pray and also watch who does it himself. I would go along and sit quite a ways away, so I don't interfere with him and watch him go through the motions. It's still done like that, it's still the same way today that we do here. The ceremony is still the same way, the singing and everything is still the same. When I grew up to three or four years of age, why I used to sing, I didn't know all the songs, but I knew some of the words. They said I used to sit on a trough and bang on the water tank and sing to the Spirits! So that's the reason I grew up to be kind of an authority on this, from watching the ceremony, because I knew somebody and I grew up with it.

When I grew up, why my Dad died, so I had to work and support my mother and my brother Raymond. After I graduated from high school, I got a scholarship, so I went to Phoenix, Arizona. I went two years there studying art, 'til I was a good artist and that's what this scholarship was about. This would be the Santa Fe Art School that used to be. Somehow they wanted a bigger school so they moved it to Santa Fe, and then I don't know what happened to the other school in Phoenix.

But I went into the service. I went to the Air Force for four years and finally got discharged in 1945. I came home and started dancing. I made my way up to the purest style of dancing that everybody liked. They were competing in dancing contests, so I did a few exhibition dances. I had about six bustles on, you ought to see them. I had two or three outfits in different colors. If there's a three day dance, they used one outfit one day, another a different color the next. But after I got married, I kept slowing down. I was still dancing, but I kept slowing down.

I got more into Indian Religion. I studied more and more as I came into contact with other Indian people like Frank Fools Crow and we talked about things and feathers and medicines and that sort of thing. My mother married three times so I had stepbrothers and one of my stepbrothers taught me how to do it. They were Medicine Men and good ones too. They taught me about these things.

(Name omitted) was the first to suggest that we take the pipe up. Just before that we went to a Sweat Lodge and asked him if he was powerful enough and if we were good enough that we could make the ceremony and we were. He said we could tell the people about their religion. He told us a few things that we had to do and we did them. One was that we had to go to a Sweat Lodge if we were going through the ceremony. All the ones that were on the committee or directors had to all go into the Sweat Lodge and purify ourselves before we could perform the ceremony. We weren't the actual performer, but we have to sweat, you know, for the medicine, but we knew that we have to do it that way. Also we're not supposed to take pictures because of the reflection and that could send the Spirits away. They're powerful; their lightning is powerful, more powerful than that, they'll kill you by the reflection.

When I was a little kid, I seen this pipe in the 1930s. I remember because it was the Depression, dust blowing every day and you have to drive around with the lights on! The cattle were just skin and bones and no water! It was really terrible. Everything we possessed was just full of sand. So I guess that these old people that had this pipe, but they wouldn't open it, regardless. That happened right here in Green Grass, they opened it for the first time. But I was small enough that I couldn't remember what it looked like. I know it was the pipe. It was a beautiful pipe, one eagle feather on it. In fact, that's the same feather that was on there when they brought it. So it must be a pretty old feather, but it's in real good shape. It had some markings, carving, all this kind of thing, rather than just an ordinary pipe. You could feel the presence of something. Even I was pretty scared. I was involved in that all the time.

Today we use the pipe for a lot of reasons. One time we prayed for the Wounded Knee to cease without any bloodshed in it. It didn't until after several people got killed. You can expect something like that. But as a whole, the people that was out there nobody was shooting like they mean it, it was more of a scare tactic. But it turned out alright, because that's the way we prayed. Anything you pray for, you got to expect it to happen.

That was 1919, I was born in. I lived there all my life, except the time I went to Arizona and then on into the service from there. I didn't come back home for six years, I think it was 1945, the first time I came back. And that's the funniest thing, I forgot my Sioux language! When I went into the house my mother was sitting there just as happy as can be and started talking to me and hugging me up. I was gonna say something and I just couldn't remember! I can distinctly remember, the communication was there, as far as that goes and I knew what she was saying, but my words couldn't come out. So it's possible to lose the language. I believe it. Like my kids, they don't speak it, they lost it. But I'm pretty sure that they could get it back if they were taught by an Indian in this. They have to be trained. Indian language teachers have to be trained.

My grandfather's name was Ray Eagle Chaser and he was about the oldest one in Cherry Creek. That's where they homesteaded and they lived along Ash Creek, where they had a ranch. They owned a lot of horses and had cattle and pigs and turkeys and chickens. They were hardworking people, you know. My grandmother, as soon as that sun comes up, she's out there doing something. Preparing a hide, or making *parfleche* bags and those are hard to make, but she does all that, tans hides, makes moccasins. In those days you don't sell them, you give them away. Like a relation comes from Pine Ridge and they stay overnight or for a couple of days. They really treated them nicely. Feed them the best food that they had, that they know how. They give them the best beads and stuff like moccasins and shawls and blankets. They don't expect nothing in return. Sometimes my grandfather will give them a horse. He looks at their horses, and if it's kind of lame, why, "Here's a couple more that you can have. They're broke to ride." So those things don't mean nothing to them, they just give them away. Just so they can make their way home they give them extra food, dried meats and extra blankets, and they take them home. They give them a lot of water before they take off back to Pine Ridge, because they might have to camp two or three times on the way before they get home. Then if we go over there, why they do the same thing to us. They might give you something, maybe not a horse, but they do quillwork, and that's a beautiful thing.

My grandmother told me later when I was able to comprehend a lot of things, that because I was the oldest son, I was in a cradle, *wokazeze,* they call it. It's beaded with porcupine needles and that's the fanciest. They hold it highest, because there's a charm in one of those things, *Woken wokazeze*, they call it. That's a cradle. It's really made nice. I had one of those, like I say. In the parades they used to have, my grandmother carried me on her back. My Indian name is *Naca Cikala,* Little Chief. "*Naca Cikala, Naca Cikala.*" She used to sing that, using my name *Naca Cikala* to let people know that, "Here's a boy! My grandson! Someday he's going to be a good boy and a good man and a leader." So I always remembered that.

My grandfather was a good one. When he smoked, when I was still small, why he gives me the pipe! He says, "Hey". So I smoked the pipe, which is something they don't do that very often. They wouldn't let anybody smoke unless they're good enough, let you smoke the pipe. So that's the way they treated me. And I always live up to it, I always try to live up to what my grandmother and my grandfather taught me. The stories, anything that they taught me, I remembered. That's the reason I'm religious, no crime. My work and my paintings are all religion. This lady at Rapid City said that, she wrote about me, "This man is a good painter, and a different style. It's all a religion basis. His paintings are all religion," that's what she said, and she was telling the truth. She said that in 1972. She hit the nail on the head.

Two - Melvin Miner
A Ceremony for his Mother

My mother was in a coma in the hospital here in Rapid City and somebody recommended this *yuwipi* man. The ceremony was down at Batesland on the Pine Ridge Indian Reservation with a *yuwipi* man name of Dawson No Horse. People said he was really good and so I went down there with some family members. We got there a little bit late too. His requirement is like a lot of them which is to sweat first. So we went ahead and sweated and I believe I might have been the only one who went into the ceremony. This *yuwipi* ceremony started after it got dark. He had a *yuwipi* house, basically a real nice place for about 100 people to fit into. It's all dark in there. They do have a light but they turn off that light during the ceremony. All the holes are covered up, any kind of cracks, no light is allowed to go into the *yuwipi* ceremony or what we would call house ceremonies.

They started the ceremony when it got dark, with an opening prayer from the Medicine Man. He explained a few things; why some people were there; where he learned; mainly things with health. Then songs were sung to call in the Spirits and then shortly after that everybody gets to pray. So it was probably 30 or 40 people before myself, so some prayers were short, some were long.

One thing I remember from this ceremony was right away there was somebody who was going up on the hill to *hanbleceya* (vision quest). He mentioned that he wanted to make a vow to fast and stay up on the hill for six nights and seven days. I have to laugh because some other people there either laughed 'cause they thought it was funny or some people thought it was courageous or some people thought it was unheard of. The standard vision quest is four days, four nights. A lot of people do one day or two or three. The maximum is four days, four nights. The Medicine Man Dawson stopped the ceremony and told him, "Not even Crazy Horse could go that many days." He told him to rethink and he's gonna go around, listen to all the prayers, then he was gonna come back to him to see if he changed his mind. So I've never heard that before or after, only time and since it's dark in there you really don't know who it is.

The prayer came around to me and I was asking for a prayer for my mother. She was in a coma. She had an operation; something went wrong there with the operation, so we didn't know how it was going to turn out. So I mainly prayed for that. As I just got done, I seen something moving towards me coming down an aisle. It looked like a midget, a little tiny man. It didn't look like a boy; it looked kind of a little bit stocky. Anyhow, I found out later it's a Spirit. I kind of knew it was at the time.

He came up to me and he took my right hand and he brushed it against his hair which was parted down the middle. One side it left open, the other side was in a braid. He brushed my hand against his hair, then across his face to the side that had a braid on it and my hand went down that full braid of hair. Then he went ahead and was grabbing me in a way to lift me up. So I stood up. Here he started to hit my legs; he wanted me to do something so I started moving them up and down. Then he hit my arms to lift them. So I lifted my arms up and then he grabbed me right in the chest area and pinched me really hard. And at that time, even though I hadn't Sun Danced before then, it kind of comes into your mind that what you are doing is Sun Dancing. I did that for a little bit and then he finally let go and he motioned to me, pulled me down to where I sat down again.

At that time a bird... I could hear the flapping. It was flapping around and it landed on my head! Its claws were very sharp and I could feel... I could feel them all over then on my head! Then I could feel the wings coming down past my ears on my shoulders and back. I could feel it! Then I could see a motion of a head coming over and a beak tapping me on the forehead several times and the wings flapping, then it flew off.

We went through the ceremony and then we went back to this guy who gave the vow of six nights, seven days. He asked him if he rethought that and he said, "Ok I'm gonna go four days and four nights." The Medicine Man was happy with that and said, "Even that is going to be tough, but I'm sure you can make it."

Then the Medicine Man said, "The Eagle landed on somebody's head. I want to speak with you after the ceremony." I knew it landed on my head. I'm not sure who else it might have landed on, or if it did or not. Well anyhow it got done and they usually eat afterwards and people were eating and visiting and I went up to him and he knew it was me. He told me, "Your mother has brain damage. The Eagle went over to the hospital and went inside. It evaluated her and said her brain is not all there. So if she lives she'll be taken care of the rest of her life with the machines or with caretakers. She won't recognize nobody. They made a mistake during the surgery to bring this on. But if you release her, then that's your family choice. Everybody should realize that by coming here to prayer that you done everything you could for her. This is what we are telling you, in six days she's going to pass away." That did come true. In six days she did pass away. He said from that night of the ceremony, "Get your relatives together there. Some might believe you, some might not. But you got six days to prepare for her death, her funeral." That was one of the instructions.

The next one was he said that he had a Spirit helper, *Cannumpa Gluha Mani* (Walks with the Pipe). This was that small kind of midget man. He said that when your hand goes on his braid that there will be certain things granted or certain things made clear to you. Interpretating back to the Medicine Man the Spirit said that he is going to do his best to help with the situation and that you're going to Sun Dance up north. Of course I never Sun Danced before, so I was a little bit worried about that.

Also he said, "My Eagle landed on your head and he wants to help you." He asked me if I remembered how that felt, with the claws going into my skull. And I said, "Yeah, it's kind of painful, irritating." I know it's something sacred so you don't move; just go with that, it's kind of a sacred moment. He said, "You can call on this Eagle at your darkest times when you need help or when you are in a bad situation. Call on him. He will come and he will be with you."

Maybe one of the reasons I think he was trying to explain this was, I lost my father at an early age and now my mother who wasn't very old when this took place. I actually became an orphan or a *wablenica*. A lot of times you have other aunts and uncles that kind of take over the role that maybe your mother or father might have had. In this case, this Eagle would be with me and if I did have problems I could call on it. So it was kind of a blessing that he gave me with that. By going there looking for help for my mother, I got some bad news. But at the same time, for doing that, they went ahead and gave me a direction and a blessing. One was to Sun Dance. The other one was that they were not going to send me into this situation or into this new world now that my mother is going without a Spirit helper and that was this *Wanbli Gleska* or Spotted Eagle.

Three - Sidney Keith
Origin of the Sun Dance

Before the Calf Pipe Woman, the Indians, they lived right. There was no alcohol. There were no bars. They knew that something made them and they looked at everything and said, "Somebody made all this around us. The animals, how come they got four legs? How come they got horns and we don't?" They figured it out that there was something more powerful than they were that did all this. So they prayed to Him, and the first Sun Dance was originated.

This one Indian, he was so dejected he went without food and didn't drink no water. He thought, "That'll kill me for sure." The fourth day he got up on the hill and he was looking at the sun, thinking and here he saw something. He saw his visions, so he put both hands up to the sun and he started dancing, while he seen that vision he danced like that. The people said, "Hey, look at that guy up there! He's crazy!" Two or three of the older people got up and they watched him from a ways.

Actually, he was praying towards the sun. He was dancing, and that's how the

Sun Dance started; because he saw a vision and that's one of God's greatest creations, the sun. It never fails. It's gotta go around, come up and go down again. So they knew that, "Oh, God created that too!" and so they're not worshipping the sun when they do that. They're praying to one of the creations by God. Hoping then that while they are praying to Him, that sun, the prayers might bounce off it, go to wherever the Great Spirit is. You can't see Him, because He's almighty too, the Great Spirit, you can't see Him. But you know He's up there, and so are the Spirits. You can't see them, but they're there.

I just remember as far back as when I can, that my grandfather used to tell the stories to do with the Sacred Pipe. So I knew, when I was able to comprehend, a lot of stories. Right there I knew that there was something sacred here that the Indians used and kept. Later on I saw a sack hanging up there in the tree and nobody bothered it. So that's the reason they kept it up high. But most of the time they kept it in kind of a coop, and you could see all those flags hanging in there. I always wanted to look in there and see. The pipe keeper, this lady's name was *Anpo*, it means Dawn, and she was kind of feeble, she was so old. Her eyes were not good. So her daughter took care of her for to see that nobody goes in there and stuff like that. So that when she died, this Mrs. Bad Warrior took care of it. And this son, whose name was Oscar; he was supposed to be in line to take it, but they didn't. This son was one of the worst guys, like any other guy who does too much drinking. This is not good. So I think eventually the son died, had a horrible death, out here just south of Eagle Butte, he's parked over there drunk so he was asphyxiated. And another relative died. His wife left two kids, and they all left, and soon after his mother died. His dad died before that, and he married again, but his wife divorced him. He was having a heck of a time! So mysteriously, all of her family, they was all gone. So next in line was this Looking Horse, the old lady, but she died soon afterwards. That left it to Stanley, and Stanley naturally gave it to the oldest son, which is how it should have been, you know. It was coming by generation to generation, but somehow back there they gave it to a woman, which they never should have done.

 The Sans Arc band was the band that was given the Sacred Pipe. Well one time all the Indians were running around this country looking for food and buffalo and deer that were pretty scarce. I guess it's kind of a cycle, that some years it's kind of bad. That's when they used to take this bundle and the Medicine Man would get out and pray, "We want to see some buffalo." This was to tell the Great Spirit that the Indian people are starving. When they go to bed one of these medicine men would be sleeping and see a vision and the vision told him what to do. Before sunup he gets up and tells the people that help him when he does his ceremonies, "Get up. Get up. We've got to do something here. I seen a vision." So they get up and here's what they do. They take this bundle out, and they take some sage, and sweet grass, you know, incense. "Before the sun comes up," he says, "the coyote's gonna come and he's gonna tell me which way to go."

Sure enough, they got up and they done that, they had the bundle out on the tripod. They were all sitting around smoking a pipe, and pretty soon you hear a coyote real soft. They look over and here there's two coyotes sitting there. Then they just yelp and just make all kind of noise you know, just like talking. They're not real ones, those coyotes. They're sacred. They're *wanagi*, the spirit of a coyote. So the coyotes told him to take the bundle over three hills and then at the fourth hill when he sees a river with a bend on it, you set the bundle right on the side of that hill. So the Medicine Man told his helpers to do that. So they walked, but they didn't walk like people normally do. They walked in a *wakan* way, in a holy way and they prayed as they went. While they were doing this, the coyotes would go out of sight, and the next hill they'd be sitting there again. This way it was the fourth time they disappeared, and that's where they were supposed to set the bundle. Over the fourth hill they saw it, kind of a creek with a lot of sage in it. So they set it there and waited a couple of days.

After the third day one of the helpers who stayed over there, he got hungry and he came back to camp and the next guy came and stayed three days. The fourth day this last guy went and checked and he seen about forty or fifty head laying around there at the tripod, you know, some of them buffalos! None of them ran or nothing! They just laid around there, just having a siesta there. So he ran back to tell everyone there were lots of buffalo.

They got the warriors with the fastest horses, those were Pawnee horses and they went out there and killed a lot of them buffalo! They got their meat! They hauled the meat back to camp and when they were bringing them back, they had their women bring the Pipe Bundle back. It was a maiden that was a virgin; she carried the Pipe Bundle back. They put sage underneath of all of it. She cried all the way back, just humbling herself. That's the way they brought the Pipe. They brought it into camp and she set it down and the Medicine Man took it and prayed again and put it back into the tent. This is a story my grandfather told me, just to show me the power that this Pipe had, generation to generation. Well this story is true.

The Pipe done quite a bit for the Indians in those days. There was no such thing as a history book said, what is it? War shirts. There was no such thing as war shirts, but the Pipe did a lot of things like that. Like these guys who count coups, they pray over this Pipe before they go on a war party. What they did, they didn't fight them soldiers, they just wanted to show how brave they were. So they knocked somebody down on the ground and they go right by them and hit them with their coup stick, just go by and yell. Four times they had to do it! So when somebody else see's them, they can say, "Well, we seen him do it." Then the chief, gives him a war bonnet, makes him a sub-chief. That's the way they come up, like your Army, you're promoted. That's where they got their prestige, there's a lot of prestige in that. Bravery is the main thing.

Four - Melvin Miner
College Days

In the mid 1970's my cousin Chuck Davis, my sister Marlyce and a friend of ours named Peggy Phelps, signed up for classes at Sinte Gleska Community College. Back then it was down on the Rosebud Reservation, right in St. Francis. We had a place (they didn't have dorms down there) so we had to stay in some houses. The house we stayed at was where a couple of Fathers who were Catholic priests lived, but they were gone for the summer. We took some classes. Victor Douville was the instructor of History. There was a guy from California; he was a non-Indian, Tom Simms. He was a teacher out in California at one of the colleges or universities out there, he came out to teach. There was Albert Whitehat who was a teacher down there. Merci Poorman, I'm not sure if she was a teacher or if she was a speaker, she spoke to us quite a bit.

That summer there was a sweat lodge right there in the St. Francis area. My cousin Chuck, me and a guy named Fred Stands, we went to a sweat lodge with the person who was running it, he was blind.

That was one of the first sweat lodges that I'd been into and it was a really good experience in there, he interpretated some prayers. The thing that I remember though was when we left from that sweat lodge and we were walking back to our place, maybe a half mile. There was an elderly lady outside of her home and she started to cry as we were getting close to her. So Fred Stands, he walked over to talk to her to see what was going on. We were standing there waiting. He came back and said what this lady seen and even though it was a clear sky out, she seen a bolt of lightning come down and hit me on top of the head! So that's why she was crying. We kind of looked at each other and said, "Wow! Something must have happened in that sweat lodge!" Maybe she seen that happening, maybe she didn't, but she was feeling bad at the time. Fred went back and explained to her that we came out of the sweat lodge and that he checked on me and I was okay and I didn't really feel nothing at that time. It was just a kind of a weird experience that came from that, being that that was my first sweat lodge.

I graduated from Rapid City High School in 1975. I went to the University of South Dakota down in Vermillion, South

Dakota and there was some racism down there. It was the first time I could see it from moving into a community. Living in Rapid City I could see racism all around me. Especially, it would flare up in the early stages of the American Indian Movement. But me coming into another community, I could see small kinds of racism. Different students would talk about what they had experienced, not necessarily at the school itself, but all around the area. People would say things about Native Americans. But you've got to remember the Wounded Knee Occupation took place in 1973, so there was a lot of tension. It was kind of a tough time to go to school.

Rosebud Reservation was doing pretty good because they started their community college there. Different reservations were picking up the idea that instead of their children and students going off to school at the universities and different colleges; that they could hopefully keep them on the reservation where their family, their support system was and provide them with a degree in their field of choice. They would also have the option of, or the benefit of, learning more about their people with native history, language courses, thought and philosophy and they would learn it from their elders, Medicine Men and people from within their community. So I think it was just starting to catch on then. It took years to get the funding for the colleges. A lot of places didn't have the buildings and facilities to house these community college or junior colleges at their home reservation.

Sometime later we went to what I call a house ceremony but it's a *yuwipi* ceremony. Robert Steed, he's from that reservation, we went to his ceremony and I'm gonna say that thirty of forty people were in there. I remember two things from that ceremony, which would have been my first *yuwipi* ceremony. First off, was there was this individual in there, this one man prayed for his leg injuries. So the Medicine Man said, "The Spirits told you to go to the I.H.S. clinic, they can fix your leg. Go to the V.A. Hospital and they can go ahead and fix this." The man, I find out later on is very unstable mentally, argued back. "Well I come here to get doctored. That's why I'm here. Can't your Spirits doctor me?" It was still dark in the ceremony, so we didn't know who it was. The Medicine Man politely said, "Well I'm just telling you what the Spirits say. You can get this help from them." The other man persistently asked for help from him and finally Robert

Steed said, "We can't help you! It's something that they told me. You have got to get help somewhere else!" Since then I have never been in a ceremony where somebody has argued like this man, who was not showing respect. But then we also found out that he had some type of mental problem that came from being in Viet Nam, so that explained it, but that was something that I have not seen since.

The other thing is that he interpreted my cousin's and my prayer. One thing that he mentioned to me was he told me I was going to live for a long time. I was pretty young at the time, probably like 18 or so. He said I was going to live a long time but he said that doesn't mean get in a car and drive over a cliff and expect to live. We kind of all laughed around in there about that. I wasn't sure why he was telling me that other than I remembered that certain situations that come up later, where it looked like it was going to be a dangerous situation; I remembered what he told me. I expected to come out of these bad situations from what he interpretated to me that day.

Down in Vermillion I had a friend and one day I went to see him. He was gone but the next door neighbor came out as I was knocking on the door. His name was

Charles Fast Horse and so I introduced myself and we talked a little bit. He said that he was living in Rapid City but he was from the Pine Ridge Reservation. So we visited for awhile. Turned out he was a Medicine Man. I went and seen him several years later in Rapid City.

At Vermillion there was an elder named Joe Rockboy and he was a spiritual leader. I believe he was from the Yankton tribe. He really was the main Medicine Man in that area. I'm not sure how many visions he has had or what kind of Spirits he worked with. He was an elk dreamer; he had a dream of an elk so he had what they call an elk dreamer medicine. It can heal but also he can dream about people or things. One of the gifts to that ability is that as you are sleeping, you will dream of something that is taking place, of somebody or some event. One day he came to see me and he wanted to talk to me. I said sure. You have to realize that during those college days I was partying, for sure on the weekends if not throughout the weekdays sometimes. I was still working out, running on the cross country and the track team. I was still in shape but I was going out a lot too. He told me that he had a dream about me and he told me some things about me that really only an elk dreamer could know. Joe, he was pretty well known in that area by the time I was down there and got to know him. It was probably 1976 or 1977; he was probably about 75 or 80, maybe even older than that at the time. He asked me too if I would help him with a Pow Wow. That was part of his dream, putting on a Pow Wow down there. So we went over to Kevin Locke (he's now a world renowned hoop dancer, flute player and performs all around the whole world) he was going to school down there. We went over there and we had a sweat lodge. I came out and I remember I was smoking this pipe, either Kevin's or Joe's pipe in Kevin's house that night. Kevin Locke was a good person to know then, I'd asked him quite a few questions about Indian spirituality but I was still kind of committed to partying.

We did a Pow Wow, it was real small. It was kind of a pitiful Pow Wow in a way. Then next year we did one that we were allowed to use the basketball arena. They didn't have a very big basketball arena, almost between a grade school and a high school basketball court with limited seating for a university. At the first Pow Wow, the one I call kind of a pitiful Pow Wow, we had about 20 dancers. I was still running track and cross country. Actually in high school I still have the record down at Central High for the two mile run and that was in 1975 and its 2009 now, 35 years almost. But at this time my mother, she had a lady friend out of Santee, Nebraska. They decided to go ahead and give me an Indian name at that time and that Indian name is *Maka Sitomni Oiyanke* (He Who Runs Around the World). We had a give away at that moment, they did the honoring song and the Pow Wow went ahead and closed that night. The next year we actually had the bigger Pow Wow. Joe Rockboy was getting up there in age and he was the announcer. Everybody felt pretty good about that. I think it was something that he wanted to do. Sometimes he had a hard time hearing; you kind of had to raise your voice to speak to him.

I remember also there were quite a few people that were going to peyote ceremonies. Peyote is a practice of the Native American Church. I don't know of that many Lakota's that participate in that but I know that there's a lot more Nakotas and Dakotas it seems like. A lot of them live on the east side of the state, living in that area, they would have their meetings. They would be all night meetings where they basically pray and sing. I told Joe Rockboy that I was invited to one. He sat me down and he said, "I personally don't want you to mix the sacred pipe with these other ceremonies, such as this peyote." He said that wasn't the way that he was brought up or that he believed for himself. He said that for others, that works for them but that he asked me if I wouldn't participate in the peyote. He said just stick with the sacred pipe. At that time I told him that I didn't have a pipe. He said, "Well, I would just prefer that you just go with this way of life with the *inipi*, the sweat lodge, without the peyote." So I never did get to participate. But several roommates and some other people that I was associated with, they would go and participate in the all night ceremony.

    The next thing I know, I was getting really sick. I was also having some bad dreams. I remember going to see this girl, I went to her home. It was on one of the reservations and I remember that I was going to eat some soup and I felt like something was wrong with it. I actually declined twice, something told me to decline twice. They were very persistent that I eat this soup. It was two ladies and it was almost like I was disrespecting them, but there was something that was holding me back from eating that soup. Usually I will eat **anything,** but I remember resisting. Finally I gave in. After I ate that soup I came back to Vermillion, it was actually a long drive.

I started having some dreams and they weren't good dreams. In the dreams, this woman I went to see was above me, over me. She reached down and put her hands around my neck, to strangle me. I could feel her hands on my throat. At one point she plucked some hair from my head.

Soon after that dream my neck began to swell up. After about a week I went to Joe Rockboy who told me to go to Kevin Locke. So I went to Kevin and said, "You know I need some kind of help. I know it was something I ate but something is happening. I'm having this dream and it's not a good dream" He said, "I'll take you down to the Medicine Man. He's kind of just starting off. His name is Robert R.L. Running, down on the Rosebud Reservation." So we went down there for a ceremony. He had a really nice *yuwipi* house, from the outside it didn't look all that good but the inside it was all painted, decorated. I remember there were a lot of eagle feathers, some hides, so it was really nice inside.

We had a ceremony that night and I prayed for this dream that I had. While I was there the Spirits and Medicine Man asked me to stand up. One reason I wasn't there for, but I'm glad that I went how was from constantly running I had some problems with my foot. We'd have to run between four to six miles in the morning and then between six and fifteen miles in the evening while running track and cross country. I had some problems with my foot that led to a problem with my knee that led to a problem with my back. I could feel that there was a pain there. There was an imbalance. I could feel it getting worse. The Spirits had me stand up and the rattle went exactly right on my foot that was hurting, went up to my knee and then went to my back. They said that they healed some things that were wrong with me.

At that time I was very impressed because that really wasn't the reason why I went there for. But also they took something off of me and they put it in a red cloth. They showed it to me and I identified it and then they took it to a small hill and they burnt it and sent it away. I knew what they interpretated to me is the only thing that could have happened:

In the dream, the woman reached down to me and pulled a hair from my head. She wrapped it around a spider. At the ceremony the Spirits and the Medicine Man pulled the spider off of me.

They also said that if I seen this person again down the road, that this person would be wearing red and I would recognize them. Several years later I saw this person that was part of this ordeal, **years** later, after they told me. Here that person was all dressed in red! I could not believe it. They also told me some things to be aware of, to watch out for. We did kind of a *wopila* (thank you) that night because we figured we would probably not be able to go down there again, so we gave some gifts. What we did that night was good enough for the *wopila*. They also said that both of us were going to school and that's what we should be doing is attending school and getting our education there.

Down in Vermillion, I remember another house ceremony. It was actually a ceremony in a building on campus with Charley Kills Enemy. Somebody asked him to come down and do a ceremony for the Indian students down on the campus. Also down there was the first time I met Arvoll Looking Horse. We went out of town to this guy's house and Arvoll was there. This guy Wayne had quite a few horses; I rode one of his horses there. I think Arvoll was down there and did a ceremony, maybe the night before. I didn't attend that ceremony but that was the first time I met him.

Five - Sidney Keith
Spirits at the Creation

The Spirits originated at the beginning of creation. The Spirits are never born, and they never die. They are there all the time. There will be a day that the Great Spirit decides to change the world and they're still gonna be there. The Indians knew how to use them. By giving us visions, the Great Spirit taught the Indians how to get the visions so we can use the Spirits. At the beginning they went around to each corner (there had to be four corners, so we can call it North, South, East, and West) and the *Iktomi* went around and helped him. They started from the West. They told the Spirits there they should pick a direction, since this is God's creation, the Earth, it's gotta be watered a certain time of the year. The Spirits of the West, the Thunder Beings and the horses, they watch that. Every summer they gotta water the whole thing. An old Indian, after it rains, a nice rain, an Indian will come up and tell them other Indians, *"Miniapapson"*. Like you'd say, "The Spirits watered the grass." We didn't do it. The Spirits did.

They went to the North and told the Spirits up there, the *Waziyata* (well in your words it's Santa Claus, he watches the weather there in the wintertime). Everything has got to be frozen, you know, you've gotta have a refrigerator to keep things cold. So all the animals know what to do during the winter, they hibernate, or they go south where it is warmer. See? They're smart. All the birds know what to do, in the spring they come back at certain times. They know what time to come back. All the Spirits watch the directions; they were made when God created the earth.

Fools Crow, he's a pretty good Holy Man. The Pipe that he has is blessed, that way he can communicate with the Spirits, and they obey him. The Spirits that we use, they are not from this earth; they're above this pollution and everything. The only way you can call on them is through the Pipe. You have to pray to them, and call them, and they'll come. Especially a Medicine Man, where he has his altar, that's where they show up and they show up by doing different things. You see a blue light, a clicking light. They stamp on the floor, if it's a deer, they stamp on the floor, and they sound like a deer. The eagle comes in and flaps around. Sometimes the deer will come in and I have many times had the deer sit on my lap. And I can feel it right here on my hand, that it's fuzzy, like a deer with hair.

The only boss of these Spirits is the one from the West, the Thunder Beings, because they do a lot of things that people see. In summer, like now, we see clouds, rains, but the only time you see them is on your vision quest. Or like I say, the *heyoka*, they can see what they are. They can see horses coming first or dogs barking. This is the reason, when we see a big cloud coming, thunder and lightning, all the horses are scared. They're kind of unsettled, and worried about something, the animals too, they pull up their tail and they run around because they know that that's a Spirit coming.

It's dangerous; the Spirits will cooperate with everything. What they do is, in this altar, if you ask them something, they say that they took whatever you ask in your mind, your brain, they take it and open it up and they look at it. That's the way that they answer, that they took your mind and look at it, if that's all possible. But that's the way they do it.

The Medicine Man can send one of these Spirits to go way off. The other day they done that, they sent 'em up to North

Dakota. It just takes one song for the Spirit to go over there and find out what's wrong and come back. Last time, we sang one song, two verses and I was listening to see if he was back and I said, "One more," so they sang one more round and he finally did come back. He picked up that rattle again and he was going around the room. So it just takes a little while to get up there and back, and look at the sick person. If there is an infection of some sort, they can tell. They do that, they open the sick persons mind and look at it. And it's always up here (pointing at his head) the sickness, you see. The brain starts a motion, a signal. So that's the reason why they open your mind up and look at it, before it gets down to all over you, they can stop it.

They use rattles when they cure people, healing the sick. They use it to touch where you hurt. They know. Maybe you're hurting down here, but when they come up and touch you, you might be hurting up here, in the head, instead of down there. It's psychological, but they know where it is, actually. So that's the only reason they use these rattles.

A real medicine rattle has to be made out of *taleja* (bladder), or the sacred ones that you see the medicine men have, the ones the Spirits bring, they bring the really old ones, are made out of hide. Inside the real ones, they have those little rocks. They don't just pick any rocks, or sand, it comes from an anthill. You take a bunch of those, a certain size and put them in, just a handful. I would say just about the size or the pit of a cherry, about that big (indicating a diameter of about 1/8th inch). A lot of times the Spirits come in and they hit it on the floor; and they hit it too hard, and it's not made right, so those things fly all over. Also, the best part, the *wagmuha* is made just with the scrotum for the top. See, they're already round and you just turn it inside out, and dry it out. Then you put your handle, there, on it, then you shave it, then you put something on and wrap it with string. That's how they do it.

Of course, when they come in to tell you, they hiss. When the Spirit came to me, I was talking Indian, I told him to go to Mobridge Hospital to see my mother. I didn't say Mobridge, but I said, "Between the North and East direction, my mother's laying in the house." But they know, the Spirits do. We were in the log house there and we were singing the song three or four times. We were supposed to sing three times, but you know, still there was nothing, no noise. They left. They went to Mobridge and we went through three songs and we didn't hear anybody roaming around again here. Well pretty soon I felt somebody walk by me. The next thing you know, you hear a clicking noise. They're back again! So a Spirit grabbed that rattle again and started. So they can send 'em out, you know, anyplace they want. He could go clear to England if he wanted to! Just sing four songs and they go over there and come back! Just like that! Unbelievable, but they do!

All animals, all the two legged and four legged and winged, because they're the ones that gonna do these things, come from the South. They come into the altar and they show themselves. You can't see them, but they can show you those sparks and noises. They can pick up the rocks and rattle them. The eagle comes down and he flies around. He makes it small, you know, so he can fly around the altar to test people. I asked him, when he was doing that, I asked him to when he was flying around me, I asked him to go and test the *wasicuns* (white men) over there. So I think the eagle was over there doing that, and when it was my turn to talk, why I asked him, afterwards asked him if they did. And Martin High Bear said,

"*Honeh-choon.* (They did)." I just want to make a believer out of you or something.

Six - Melvin Miner
Melvin Leaves College

In 1980 I went back home to Rapid City and my mother passed away and that's where I ended up going to Dawson No Horses ceremony. Actually my cousin Chuck, he's about four years older than me, was staying there at my Mothers house when I decided not to go back to school, even though I was only short 22 or 23 hours. I decided to stay in her home and we lived out in Lakota Homes for a long time. I decided to take over on her house and also she had a vehicle, so I got to keep the vehicle.

Shortly after that I ran into Charles Fast Horse again, so I went to his house. I met his whole family and his brother Doug. Their mother was still alive, Elizabeth Fast Horse. He had quite a few sisters, Zelda, Marie and of course there were some spouses around. There were some other relatives; they had some children, Joe and Tom, Jody's brother Dave. They would be doing lots of arts and crafts; beadwork was the center of it. They would make quite a few different items. They were going to sweats quite a bit, so I started jumping in. I went to quite a few sweats with Charles Fast Horse. They would sweat every week, maybe even a couple of them, so we did a lot of sweats.

In September of 1980, my cousin Chuck and me went up to the Bismark Fair. I was up there and I was partying. The next morning I felt really sick, I wasn't sure why. I told my cousin, "You know, I'm gonna quit drinking." Something didn't feel right. So he went, "Yeahhh. Sure. Riiight." A short time later I came back to Rapid City and went to a sweat lodge with Charles Fast Horse. I vowed for one year to give up drinking, which I never thought I would do. About a month later, my cousin Chuck went ahead and made the same vow. Since we were living in the same house, we could kind of support each other in that. We still had a lot of relatives and friends that came over. We didn't enforce the no drinking policy, we just hoped that they respected our decision not to drink and eventually it kind of died down. Shortly after that I met my first wife, Sandy and I convinced her to quit drinking. I told her how I did it and so we started dating and then in June of 1981, that's when I met Sidney for the first time.

In 1981 I met my first wife, Sandra Keith. Several months later, they had a Pow

Wow up in Spearfish. She wanted me to go up there and meet her father and mother, that's Sidney and Shirley Keith. We went up to Spearfish and we met him and we had lunch together. I met him and he was real quiet. He didn't say too much, just shook my hand. We talked a little bit, I can't remember exactly what. The mother was more talkative to her daughter. We stayed up there for the day and took in the Pow Wow. That was at the Black Hills State University up there.

When I first met Sandy she didn't tell me that her father was a Medicine Man until way later. I didn't hear of him and then she mentions later on that he's a spiritual leader, does ceremonies and runs a Sun Dance. That summer in August, Sidney would sponsor a Sun Dance. Sandy was telling me about this and I said, "You know what? I was told that I should Sun Dance up north from Pine Ridge. And this thing with meeting you and your dad runs a Sun Dance. I'll talk to him." I went ahead and told him that I wanted to Sun Dance. I had been sober for a year, drug free for a year and also I told him of the ceremony I went to a year before that.

He told me that I could dance if I wanted to, but that he wanted me to be a helper. Which of course I didn't know what a helper is. He told me he had the Sun Dancers and as the spiritual leader he had to have these helpers or intercessors. They are the ones that help run the inside of the Sun Dance, the inside bowery activity around the Sacred Tree. They help lead the dancers in the different directions. They will assist or perform the piercing that goes on. They control pretty much everything in the middle. There are the sacred pipes out there. The sage that needs to be burned as smudging is going on all the time. They are getting communications from the Sun Dance leader all the time and they would have to perform that duty. I said, "Okay, I'll do that."

There were several of us, probably five of us that were the helpers. I'm not sure how other people viewed that. Some who were dancers there for a long time were probably wondering where I even came from. But a couple of things I had going for me was I was an enrolled member in the Cheyenne River Tribe. I do have a large family at Cheyenne River Reservation even though just a small handful from my *tiospaye* up there practiced this religion. They are pretty much cowboys and ranchers and law enforcement officers. Even though quite a few of them speak the language and live on the reservation they just chose not to live this way. The other thing I had going for me was that I was in shape for it. I ran almost every day for ten years before I came to the Sun Dance. I ran cross country track both in high school and then college and even after college.

Every once in a while I will say Sidney, but I really mean my father-in-law. I 'm supposed to address my in-laws as my father-in-law and mother-in-law and not their names. I'm not really supposed to address my mother-in-law or talk to her, it's just a custom and there's meaning behind that.

The bike rally only comes around once a year and has been around for a long time but Sidney used to talk about it a lot. One time before the bike rally he said a lot of times he would have the Sun Dance during the same time as the rally. There was quite a few reasons for that, spiritual reasons. But he would always make a few comments about the bike rally. He would say, "The bike rally isn't really a place for spirituality. That's why we can't go up on Bear Butte or *hanbleceya* at different places during that time. There's going to be a lot of bikers around. A lot of drinking, maybe drugs, not everybody, but a lot of them. Everybody's wearing black and that's what we wear for death. That's the color that they choose." He didn't like that but that's the color that all the bikers wear is black. Of course I'm sitting there listening to him and I'm wearing a black Sturgis Rally T-shirt. *Laughs*. I think he was hinting around to me a little bit. *Laughing*. But that would be about the inconvenience during the rally for Bear Butte and where most bikers that did go visit Bear Butte were probably pretty respectable, he just didn't like the fact that some would go up there, that were using alcohol or drugs and going onto sacred land and that it did need protection during the time of the rally.

Before I could Sun Dance I had to *hanbleceya* so in the summer of 1981, I asked Sidney to put me on the hill. When I came back down, one of the interpretations was that basically, because I dropped out of school, I had to make a living. They said the Spirits were going to guide me with the arts and crafts and that if I chose to go that way, that the Fast Horse family plus the Spirits would keep on teaching me on making traditional items and that I would be okay that way. Then I could also participate in ceremonies whenever they took place.

Sometimes in an 8 to 5 job, you can't leave or you can't get off to leave for a Sun Dance to help out, but because I was doing arts and crafts I had that flexibility. So I ended up going up to Green Grass that year, I went ahead and became an intercessor.

Sidney grew up in a small community on Cheyenne River Reservation, around Bear Creek. He was telling me that as a small child he used to go visit where this house was, this keeper of the Sacred Pipe, Martha Bad Warrior. He would go over there at different times of the day, but he would say if they were over there early in the morning she would get up with the sunrise and sing a song. Then she would burn the sage, smudge the house and the Sacred Pipe and she had to do this through winter time also, year round. And at high noon she would do it again and sing a song. They would feed the Spirits, put out food throughout the daytime or whenever they were eating. He didn't really understand all that and he said he just kind of knew things were different over there, that she would be doing these things. She would have visitors coming to see her and things like this. He said at that time, "I didn't know it, but in my heart, I realized that was a teaching for me on the spirituality of the Sacred Pipe."

He said, "The memory is real clear to me. I remember it today as one of the most respectful memories that I can remember. How important that was for us as a people." So he shared that story with me. He shared quite a few.

My wife Sandy and me, we married in December of 1981 and for a time there we lived with the Fast Horse *tiospaye*. They taught Sandy how to do beadwork. She was singing songs, her mother was a singer. Her father definitely knew the songs and would teach her some. Also around that time was the first time that Charles Fast Horse met Sidney the father-in-law.

That reminds me, that's where I did get my first pipe from, the Fast Horse family. They taught me how to load it, basically how to put the tobacco into it. Starting with the West direction, the North, the East, the South, then Above and then the last one, Mother Earth. They taught me how to wrap it in sage, take care of it and went over a lot of the rules with it, since I did have a woman with me. So that's where I received my first pipe from.

My wife and me we both were living with the Fast Horse family and had been there for several months. While we were living there I remember another Medicine

Man came there, his name was Martin High Bear and he's from Cheyenne River, the tribe. He was traveling around; living in the west coast I believe Oregon or Washington State. He'd spend a lot of time up there. We had a ceremony with him. That was my first encounter with Martin High Bear. He was the one who put up both Charles and Doug Fast Horse on the hill. Charles basically became a spiritual leader from that time that he came down from the hill. So Martin stopped in to visit. He spent maybe a day or two visiting and then he moved on. I think he was going to Cheyenne River on his trip.

One time Sandy's dad was going to come down to Rapid City from Eagle Butte and we said well we would like to have you meet Charles. Sidney had a room up in Rapid City, I can't remember the motel. We got Charles to go up there and Charles and him met. They did pretty much all their speaking in Lakota, so we didn't fully understand everything that they were saying. But they were talking about the Black Hills, different ceremonies, different things that people were doing. Towards the end of the conversation, Charles acknowledged that there was an elk spirit standing behind Sidney and he wanted Sidney to give a prayer. At the same time

Sidney acknowledged that there was a spirit behind Charles and of course we couldn't see nothin'. They both gave a prayer. We stood up; one of us gave a prayer, the other one spoke of some things that were happening. They both spoke about Sandy and myself, trying to help us, trying to get us on the Red Road, so it was a pretty good meeting from that.

Then shortly afterwards we moved back to my home in Lakota Homes. My cousin and a couple people were living there. We moved into our place and a few years after that the father-in-law and mother-in-law moved down from Cheyenne River where they had pretty much spent all their life. They had six daughters, Sandy, Alta, Jerry, Janet, Debbie and Sydney and one son, Austin, (they lost a son, Johnny) and one by one they were all moving down to Rapid City. So him and his wife moved down with us, they were seeing if it was going to work out if they liked Rapid City or not and if so they would get a place down here.

One time up there visiting the father-in-law and mother-in-law there was another Medicine Man and his name was Pete Bear Stops. He was an elderly gentleman, kind of slim built, dressed Western. He was going to have a ceremony one night, a house ceremony at his home. All the widows and everything is all covered up and it's late at night. We probably started about 10 o'clock or so. They have singers and the Medicine Man performs the ceremony. We had this ceremony with one of the medicine men other than the father-in-law Sidney. The next day, I was asking the father-in-law about Pete. He said when he was starting off Pete knew quite a few songs so he said he would buy some groceries and help him out for Pete teaching him these ceremonial songs. So I know that he gained quite a few of his songs through this Pete Bear Stops.

I remember one time that Sidney called over to the house and he said that the police were at his house in Rapid City. Usually in the summer time, especially before the Sun Dance, he would get a lot of visitors, but mainly a steady flow before the Sun Dance. Some neighbor called the police and said there's been a lot of activity throughout the year at this house, some Indian people live there and maybe there's a possibility of somebody selling drugs at the house. So a couple of police officers came over there and talked to him. Of course he was kind of defensive and he was somewhat mad that he could be accused of that. His wife explained to them that the spiritual man helps out a lot of people, so a lot of people come.

This was one of the things that he didn't like about the city, Rapid City, was that he didn't expect them to understand people coming over to visit, but back home on the reservation this was quite normal. He was upset and he got word to Rosalie Little Thunder and told her about it and she went to the city and either to the Police Department or to the mayor. But he did have a lot of traffic, out in Lakota Homes they wouldn't have been viewed that way, people, even non-Indians that lived in Lakota Homes knew about medicine men or this type of visitation with elders. Sidney lived more in a white district but that didn't stop him, he didn't tell any visitors to stop coming over or anything. He would say, "You need help? You want to visit? You come on over." He wasn't gonna change. The other people had to learn or understand this. So it was kind of funny and sad, but he was offended by this.

I remember I was telling Sidney there were a lot of magpies by my house. I actually put some buffalo skulls outside that still had some flesh on them; I got them from Custer State Park. I went up there and bought them and I brought them back and I put them up on the roof of my house. I got up one morning and boy I noticed there were all kinds of birds around and I seen some magpies. So I told him I had to take down those skulls because it was attracting too much activity even though I'd like to have the birds come and eat off that meat and stuff. I still lived in the housing district and somebody's gonna say something like I got something dead over there or something. So I was telling him about it and he said, "You know up on the reservation, there's a time when we didn't have refrigerators and times were tough. But if we seen a magpie sitting on a house, we knew that there was fresh meat at that house, they would smell that meat. We knew who had fresh meat, so if you were hungry, you would go visit. But the same worked for us if we had fresh meat at our house. We'd have visitors come over and everybody shared that way. But the magpies were giving the clues for that."

Also he said, "Sometimes we would tease somebody. The nests of the magpies were really dirty. Sometimes they would go to the bathroom inside their nests, just real messy, smelly, sometimes. If somebody lived that way, didn't take care of their house and stuff, somebody would say, 'What are you? Trying to live like a magpie or something in here?' You should clean up or something." He said that if you got teased like that you better clean up your house really quick!

Seven - Sidney Keith
Origin of the Pipestone

At one time or another, God put in a red stone on this earth. Remember back to Noah and the Big Flood? That was Noah's time. That was when there was water running all over the Earth. Then the water was receding and there was a big rock sticking up. All the water was running fast and all kinds of animals were going by, blood was streaming. This whole rock was standing up, stuck up out of the water. It was catching the blood, and the blood kept soaking into this great big stone. That's what they always tell, that's the sacred quarry where all the pipestone comes from. That was over in Minnesota. That's what they call it now, pipestone. The stone, red stone, that's all made out of blood, it turned red and hard. They found it and dug it up, and that's what they gotta use for the pipes, because of the blood, and the Spirits don't like blood. They're scared of it, because of that.

The Lakota name for a tobacco bag is *cantojuha* (heart, container). *Ojuha* means that it's usually beaded or quilled. It can be made into any kind of shape they want to design, but mostly the ones that the chiefs and the old people carry are beaded and quilled. The ones that the Medicine Men use are just plain bags, and they're buffalo hide, or deer hide. The stem of the pipe has to stick out of the pipe bag, and it has to be dismantled, the pipe has to be dismantled, to go into the pipe bag; that's the law.

The pipe tamper is called *cannumpa icasloke* (pipe, to clean it), and it's just to tamp the tobacco, and keep the fire going in the pipe. That's kept inside the bag. We use the short, straight ones; some can get really fancy. It's usually made out of hard wood, so that it doesn't burn too much. You have to use a tamper. We still use it now.

The black pipe, it's called *cannumpa sapa*. It's a little different than the red stone. Most of the Medicine Men use the *cannumpa sapa*, rather than the regular. That's hard to tell where they get the stone. Some say that the Spirits bring these pipes to them, the good Medicine Men. They're layin' all over the place, and the Spirits find them, and return them to the Medicine Men. They know where to get it, but they won't tell people where to find this black pipe stone, because it's more sacred than the red one. The *cannumpa sa* (red pipe), you can make your own; anybody can make one for the hell of it. That's what you have in most of the pipes *inyan sa* (red stone).

You can make it a Sacred Pipe and after it's blessed, you should separate it. Don't ever display them with the pipe together. You should store it with sage in the bowl. *Cannumpa iyuhaha izitka* (pipe ornamented to smoke) refers to a stem and bowl that's really fancied up. Some stems are more intricate, some have balls carved in them. Usually those are just for the show. Most of us have the quillworked ones. They usually have a deer tail from the Black Tail Deer on there, or horse tail in different colors. Any pipe can be used to pray with but it's simple to have a little L pipe shape just to pleasure smoke it.

Anything that's animal on there, someone has a vision, why they have it carved on there for you to see. You could have a bear pipe, that's for a Medicine Man to use with the Bear Spirit. The Bear Spirit is for healing. My wife has an eagle, looking right at you, and the eagles face is a little cross. He drilled two little holes, and he left the holes for when you're smoking the pipe, the eyes are red. The eyes light up. It's kind of cute.

Cansasa is found down here at Bear Creek, past Cherry Creek, you can find it. There's quite a few there. We got a guy down there that cuts it up, barks it, dries 'em up and brings 'em over here and sells it. That's how we get ours. *Cansasa* should only be cut when it's cold. In the fall or winter you can cut it. You shouldn't cut it after First Thunder, that's very important. It's the *Wakinyan's* food, the *sota* (smoke), is the reason.

The sage that we use is growing along the river. They call them *peji to waste* (grass, blue, good) or *peji to swuwela* (grass, blue, soft). The ones we see out on the prairie are big thick ones that stand about three feet high: those are not the ones. The ones that we want is the ones that has the smell. Those are the ones the buffalo used to roll over, to keep themselves acceptable to Wakan Tanka, because of the smell. When they do that, why, they're sacred, they're *wakan*, you see. That's the reason that we have to use it to stand on when we hold the pipe, so that it'll be acceptable to the Great Spirit. There are different kinds, the ones that the stem is a long, straight stem. Usually the leaves are soft. The ones you find on the prairie are stiff; it usually breaks off easy. There's just the stem after you break them off.

And there's also *wanagi peji hota* (spirit, grass, grey). We don't use that. That's for *Wanagi*, the Spirits: that's theirs. They usually have a little yellow flower, the same as *tinpsila* (prairie turnips). There's *wanagi tinpsila* that has this yellow flower: we don't touch them. Good *tinpsila* has a real long stem. Yellow is no good, you get sick. They've got a little, two three inches *tinpsila*, a skinny one. You eat that and sometimes you go deaf, or you get dizzy. I don't know what it would do if you eat a bunch of them.

Eight - Melvin Miner
A Pow Wow for Rapid City

It was some years later, after Sidney and Shirley moved down from Eagle Butte, that we noticed that the Pow Wows in Rapid City were basically just sponsored or put on by organizations for maybe a one day Pow Wow. Rapid City has a very large Indian population, it's almost eight or ten per cent of Rapid City, which at that time was probably about sixty thousand, so we probably had about five to six or seven thousand mainly Lakota people that live here. I was thinking about starting a Pow Wow and that thought carried on over from 1977 or '78 in Vermillion where I helped sponsor two Pow Wow's. Some years ago, maybe twenty to thirty years ago, there were some good Pow Wow's that were put on here, but then the next year there might not be one, so it was not like an annual thing.

So I visited quite a few people, I would say ten people. I was trying to understand the history of Rapid City on the Pow Wow scene. Every house I visited they would give me a reason why a Pow Wow might have not worked in the past or the good things that happened at the Pow Wow or the location or who put it on. They told me too: I'd go to one person's house, they would say, "You know what? This guy would know something about a Pow Wow. He has a lot of experience with being a dancer. He traveled all around. He could probably answer some of your questions. He was a championship dancer back in his days in the 60's." ***He*** was a relative; his name was Sonny Richards. Though I knew he was my relative I didn't really know him. I hadn't been introduced to him formally. So I went over there and we struck up a friendship. He gave me a lot of encouragement on the Pow Wow. He gave me a lot of history about the Pow Wow scene here in Rapid City. It seemed like they were all short lived. A year or two maybe and there would be gaps of a year or two. He said a lot of people would come, but it was just something that either didn't make money or that person for some reason or other couldn't carry it on the next year. Sonny was a Medicine Man; he trained under Chief Frank Fools Crow. Also Sonny's mother was a Medicine Woman or a spiritual woman. She had a Spirit or maybe two that worked with her. Before her death I went over there several times and spoke with her on different matters.

I went back to my father-in-law and this whole process was probably months that went on and I told him I was thinking about a Pow Wow here in Rapid City. He said, "I think that's a really good idea. In order to do that, the name of it would probably be The Black Hills Pow Wow. You know that is a sacred name. Anything like Black Hills or Bear Butte or White Buffalo Calf, these are sacred names. This is a huge undertaking. We'll do a ceremony for this and we'll see what the Spirits say." So I'm gonna guess this is probably '84 or '85.

So we went up to a home in Hill City, for a house ceremony. We set up the altar and I asked the Spirits if they could give me an answer or help me with this Pow Wow. So he gave me back the interpretation. What the Spirit said was we could use the name Black Hills Pow Wow and also that they would help me to invite other people to help develop a board of directors. He said it would run even smoother, if we had some non-Indians on the board and the Spirits would be very helpful to make sure of this. 'Cause there's a lot of doors to be opened up. There are a lot of people, businesses, politicians that don't really know what a Pow Wow is all about and they would help, these non-Indians on the board. He said there could be two, three, four whatever you want. Also there were a couple other conditions to this Pow Wow. I remember one was to make sure it would be very successful I would have to *hanbleceya*, go up on the hill, like Bear Butte or somewhere like that. I would have to go up there for so many days to ensure that I was committed to this. Also, he said once this takes off, this is gonna be big. It's gonna take a lot of work, a lot of commitment to it. I remember that one of the conditions was I would have to come back in a year and do a *wopila* right after the Pow Wow. So I agreed to these conditions.

So we got a board together, I actually put an ad in the paper and maybe three non-Indians answered that ad. I think we ended up with maybe four on the board and then we had a board of maybe five or six Native Americans. Then we started off and we had a small Pow Wow to start off with. "How pitiful" I thought. Maybe it was an educational experience for some of them who weren't familiar with a Pow Wow.

We invited business people and the mayor, politicians, different people and actually the next year we moved into the Rushmore Plaza Civic Center and that really started to take off then. But each year that I was president of the Black Hills Pow Wow I had to go up on the hill to give thanks for the year before and also to offer prayers for the coming year. We thought this Pow Wow culturally would bring something to Rapid City.

We did the Black Hills Pow Wow and we had Sidney announce for several of those years. Then we would bring in another announcer. We'd have two announcers working the Pow Wows. We did a lot of things at the beginning of the Pow Wow to ensure that it was run correctly. We always asked the Spirits to look over this Pow Wow that we would be having and we would be told quite a few things to be aware of or to look out for. So we've always had some spiritual guidance there for the protocol, the steps to it. An important step to it was having a ceremony in the Black Hills asking to use that name and also have the Spirits guide us or make this happen kind of in a timely way. It could of took years maybe, and it took less than that. Even though it's more of a social event, the Pow Wows have a lot of tradition in there, a lot of culture. Everything is brought into that arena. There are a lot of eagle feathers there, the songs, all those things are there. You can compare it to the Sun Dance and the Sun Dance is almost totally spiritual but the Pow Wow has spiritual aspects to it also. It's good to have a Medicine Man helping with the Pow Wows that you have in your community.

So we solved an issue in Rapid City by organizing the Pow Wow and we saw how that has helped our community. It served many purposes but one of them was to serve as public relations with Rapid City's non-Indian community, to say that we have something we would like to share. Another one would be to open our culture for you to come into and see. A lot of times people see our Indian people here in Rapid City walking around on the streets or they hear something bad or read something bad in the paper and they start to develop this negative image of us. We were hoping that one of the aspects of this Pow Wow would be to have the non-Indian even participate. We really needed the help for sure, financially, to help us with sponsorship. I mean we had Indian organizations also helping us but we did need non-Indians help.

The Black Hills Pow Wow is still going on 23 years later. I was president of the Pow Wow for five years then stepped down. Randy Ross took over, a really good friend. He was brought in on the early stages; he had the writing skills, plus a desire to see this thing happen. I had about seven or eight board members and we all stuck together for at least five years and even more. It just kind of wore me out after awhile, the work for the Pow Wow there are a lot of things that go on with a huge Pow Wow. You could attend a meeting everyday if you wanted to and sometimes I did.

Nine - Sidney Keith
Sun Dance Story

Eventually I can run the Sun Dance, but it's gonna take a long time. I've gotta be a Medicine Man before I can do that. But this year I'll get the chance to pierce 'em, you know, pierce their skin, tie 'em up and do a lot of things that only Fools Crow himself can give the authority to do. That's where you learn everything, being the Medicine Man, you do many things eventually and you've got to do it right too at the Sun Dance. It's not a program that you tour or a stage show or something! You've got to follow the advice of the Spirits, especially of the West.

Like last time, on the last day before the Sun Dance, Fools Crow and us, we went into the sweat lodge. He was praying he wants the Sun Dance to go right. The Spirits will all come help us, and they told him they'll all be there. The six directions watch him. He asked the Spirits over here that, "We want four good days to do this." So they say, *"Wowahwa, wowahwa lo* (Peaceful)."

So the third day it was cloudy, threatening rain. I went over to Clarence's, he usually does all the cooking there, getting all the food together and stuff. I said, "You better get your food in, and we'll go down there. I have a lot of confidence it might not rain. We should just as well get down there right away." We were tired! He said, "Okay, I'll go down there. I got all my equipment and buffalo skulls." Mark took me down there and dropped me off. I had a portable loudspeaker and set it up. I hollered out and here everybody came running, and they were all dressed to go. Eight o'clock in the morning! It was still kind of chilly, you know, but just right for a Sun Dance. Here comes Fools Crow. He's all dressed up, decked out in his outfit. He looked around, *Ho Wanna,*" he said, "I'm ready."

We had them all lined up. We had the drummers get on the ball, and they all sat down. So Clarence came and I said, "Make some coffee, a lot of it." 'Cause it was windy and kind of chilly, and they were all pretty much naked, dressed for the Sun Dance. By the time Fools Crow was coming, it looked like it would clear up; it was kind of partly cloudy. By the time you heard the first drumbeat, it seemed like it was getting wider and wider, and you could see more blue sky! I had to carry that buffalo skull when they come in, I was walking second, behind and on the right hand side of Fools Crow, and I had that skull. We go inside on the left side and line up and I offer the skull to the four directions, then I set it down. Then he prays, he goes up to the center pole and prays. I started beating on a drum, the first song and they started dancing and blowing the whistle. There were just a few clouds going by! Pretty soon it's just as hot as can be! By the afternoon, some of them are so thirsty; they just say "Water!" then just keel over.

    We had two Medicine Men. My brother Ted, Ted Bison, he was a Medicine Man, he was all dressed up. He had two great big buffalo hides on the side of him, and people come, if they wanted to and stand on this buffalo hides. He does his thing, he has a feather and a rattle and he prays and he makes the offering. He just pushes everything down and he goes like that (gesturing) and they walk away happy. His son was doing the same thing, so there are two lines of people. All had some kind of sickness. It is really something to watch. He sends them off if there is something else real wrong. He makes them dance and he pushes them towards the center pole, stands them up against it like that and he asks them what's the matter, where it is or whatever it is that's wrong.

This one guy had something in his stomach that was bothering him for many years. I just happened to stand by there and I was talking to Fools Crow asking what kind of procedure he's gonna use. So I just had to stand there while he was doing that. He said, "The doctor said I have a stone in there." "*Hau*," Fools Crow said. He put his whistle in and he was whistling and dancing back a ways. Four times he looked like he charged him. Then he'd shake his head and then he'd go back, four times. About the sixth or seventh time, he runs up to him and grabs him around the waist, puts his mouth on there and he sucks on it, two or three times. Then he hit him in the back and he took something out of his mouth and showed it to the sun. It was something, boy! He just shows it and blows his whistle, then he took it under the post in the dirt and made a little hole and put it there and covered it up. Then the old man is so happy, you know, he just starts bawling! So Fools Crow helped him up and he made him dance. He danced it for a while and he just walked away. That's the power that they have, these Medicine Men.

The weather turned out real nice! By Friday it got so hot! I was praying that it would get hot, too 'cause this is the last day and I told everybody, "Get with it! Give it all you got! We want it as hot as we can get it, so that you suffer and whatever you were doing it for, you will get it!" Each one has a different idea of what they want. He doesn't tell us why he's dancing. He doesn't tell the Medicine Man why he's dancing. But for himself, he knows what he wants, maybe to cure a sickness. Some of them are college boys and they probably want to finish college. You ask the Great Spirit for wisdom, stuff like that. Everybody, all the women dancing, they all have something they want.

They all pierce too on top of their suffering and that hurts. Man, that thing hurts! It sticks under their skin, like this. Tie a string around there and you have to run backwards and that pulls out. The women give flesh. They stick a needle through there and take a knife and cut that off. I did that, I offered sixteen of them, eight on each side. I walked off blood running down my arm. It felt good, you know, to offer my flesh. But the Sun Dance is good and powerful. Let everybody, whatever they pray for, let's hope that the Great Spirit will grant them their wish, that's what they're praying for. That's why I offered my flesh, too.

At the Sun Dance the Spirits they're there and they take the offering after you bury that flesh in the ground, mostly from that Spirit that is underneath the ground. You distribute it around, make it even. So I gave 16, eight on each side. 16 to all the Spirits divided into equal numbers. Just so it's even, two here, two there, two and two. Or you can give just one. Some of the people go high as 100 with 50 on each side, blood running all over. Fools Crow gave some on the soles of his feet. I know that hurts! That's why he did it that way, took his shoes off so they gotta cut his foot. Then he walked around. You gotta be humble yourself or suffer with the Spirits and they'll help you. You've got to humble yourself. That's why Indians get humble.

Ten - Melvin Miner
Melvin's First Sun Dance

My first Sun Dance was really hot. I was out there all day long and it was ninety degrees on this first Sun Dance. I really got sunburned but you just kind of work your way through it, then deal with the pain every day. Then after the Sun Dance you deal with the sunburn. My skin is light so I took a severe beating from the sun though it seemed to not really bother me in a sense. I would feel like I was running a fever and I was very thirsty, not so much hungry but very thirsty. But there is a lot there that keeps you motivated to continue on, knowing that you are helping the people, you are helping the ceremony, that there are a lot of prayers.

There are a lot of good things involved in the ceremony. You become more connected to the four directions, the Sun, Mother Earth; your relatives, the four legged, the winged, even what they call the green relatives our root relatives and even the water relatives. Because the water, you value that through these four days even though you don't get to see very much of it, you want it. So it becomes a major part of your thinking. It's the largest sacred ceremony we have out of the seven. In the olden days the whole tribe, the camps, the different bands would get together for the annual Sun Dance. It was a big thing. So I made it through that one and from then on (I was married to my wife for thirteen years) I participated as an intercessor all those thirteen years.

We had a lot of different helpers there. Some of them are well known in Indian Country. Along with my father-in-law Sidney Keith as the head spiritual leader, his spiritual brother was Frank Fools Crow, he would always be there. In hindsight, we had two very powerful medicine men running this ceremony giving guidance, giving their wisdom and the Spirits that they both worked with were there making sure that this Sun Dance would be a success. I felt very comfortable that I was in those two peoples hands. Frank had a helper, Vine King, who traveled around with him and helped him. Also there was another helper who spoke, interpretated for him. He was a real respected elder and Mathew King was his name. He would talk in between rounds and when we were resting because nobody is allowed to talk on the microphone while we are dancing, but when the dancing is over then the mic is left open.

The International Sundance name means basically that they wanted to make it well known to other tribes that they're welcome to come and participate. So that's why they put the International name on it. My father-in-law Sidney Keith had a group of men that were his council that overseen the Sun Dance and actually I'm thinking he might have been incorporated.

The Tree Day is usually on a Wednesday and the Sun Dance usually goes Thursday, Friday, Saturday, and Sunday. They choose a cottonwood tree to go in the center. It's planted in the center for the ceremony and it's in the middle of a circle, the four directions. The cottonwood tree that was cut down, it gave its life. We bring it into the Sun Dance to replant it. It is still alive through the ceremony but it knows it has an end coming. It's just like when we get ready for a funeral. When somebody dies we try to bury them within four days so that the spirit is still there, until we complete the ceremony for the one who passed away. The same way here with this tree, it's gonna live until we get done with that ceremony so its spirit is still there within the tree.

The drums are there to provide the music and the sacred songs. Then you've got the sacred supporters. The leader, the Sun Dance leader is usually sitting by the drum. There is usually a microphone and he speaks. Other people are allowed to come up and say a few words. The buffalo dancers are the ones who are the ones who are in charge of doing the cleansing, the smudging. They call it *azillia,* which means to smudge. They are bringing around the metal pots that are usually old coffee cans with smoldering sage, sweet grass and some cedar inside

The morning of the first day the leader of the Sun Dance (in this case it would be Sidney) would bring out the Sun Dancers. We would line up outside of the bowery facing the West. When we are all lined up they blow an eagle bone whistle and a prayer is given asking for a good day and for the Spirits to watch over the ceremony, for health and for a good life. The Spirits listen to our prayers. What we call the first medicine people or Spirits were made in the West. We usually pray to the West direction first. Each of these four brothers was placed in a different direction and they actually established the directions in our creation stories.

A lot of times the Sun Dance is about giving thanks for the previous year or years and so it is about giving a *wopila* or thanks. You are also praying for the children, elders, people who need help and any personal issues you have with your family, your job, marriage, relationship problems, they could be good or bad. You could give thanks for some good things that are happening. Or if you got some difficult things going on in your life then you are asking for some intervention, some help. At the same time we're thinking about creation, so in the prayers you would thank the Great Spirit, the Four Directions and the Eagle above and Mother Earth. You would ask them to listen to your prayer and then you would thank the Spirits since they were here first before us. Then you would thank your ancestors who developed this ceremony and then carried it on so that we could have this day and thank them that this ceremony is still active. So we give thanks to them. The opening prayer is really important for that.

We begin to move when that opening prayer is done. We will stop four times before we get to the East entrance which is the pathway or the doorway into this ceremony. So we stop four times and blow our whistles and there is a short prayer each time. The father-in-law is in the front carrying a buffalo skull and that's for a couple of reasons. Buffalo is our closest four legged relative which provides food, shelter, tools, everything for us. We could probably make two or three hundred items from the buffalo. It was very valuable to us. There were plenty of buffalo so they assisted us as a people throughout the thousands of years. So we have that symbol, the buffalo skull for the buffalo and also for the White Buffalo Calf Maiden. They say between seven hundred and one thousand years ago that she came upon Mother Earth and even though nobody knows for sure, a lot of people feel that she came to us somewhere between Devil's Tower and Bear Butte, probably closer to Devil's Tower. That's the name that's used now. The Bear's Lodge is one of the names that we use for that sacred site.

    So the father-in-law would carry the buffalo skull in and it's also associated through the creation with *Wi* (the sun). The buffalo is somebody or something that is in almost all our ceremonies. If it's the buffalo skull or the buffalo robe or different pieces of the buffalo horn which we use in the sweat lodge that's associated with *Wi-* the sun, it's a connection there, like a relative, a four legged relative to the sun. The buffalo skull has many meanings.

As we enter through the East gate each dancer turns in a clockwise circle once as you're going through that door, before entering the Sun Dance Altar. Then you head to the South direction, the South gate and then you dance to the West, then you go to the North. Then a lot of times you will head straight from the North door to the Sacred Tree in the middle of the arbor and then continue on to the South door. There will be one line and the intercessors will be right behind the leader and then the dancers, the male dancers, then the female dancers will follow. Sometimes you can make one large line; maybe you might have to make two, with the second line basically being the women. So when we do this it's kind of the opening ceremonies.

From the South door, we are all lined up facing East and we are welcoming the Sun. We are letting the Sun know we are there for this ceremony. We are going to direct our prayers towards the Sun and towards the Sacred Tree and also the directions. We are going to develop that relationship, that connection. Some stories are that when the Great Spirit created everything that He gave everything of Himself, because He is a giving person, a loving person. In doing that this creation is all from Him, from Him physically, His energy. In the end He gave so much that He became hard like a rock. So a lot of times we recognize that and teach that. When they bring the stones into the sweat lodge, somebody might say, 'Bring in the *tunkashila*' or 'Pour water on the *tunkashilas.*' That's part of Him, that he gave so much. But part of that is also the Sun. Some recognize the Sun as a visible burning heart of the Great Spirit. We see His heart; it gives the warmth, the light and security from His heart. It's visible and we should not question it, it's always there. This also describes a person's heart. You can't live if you don't have a heart that is healthy. In this case we know that the Sun gives energy to every living thing, it gives that energy, that warmth to grow or to be healthy. We sometimes were told that during the Sun Dance just to refresh that concept in our minds.

When we do that opening prayer inside the altar we are carrying our Sacred Pipe *Cannumpa Wakan* during this prayer welcoming the sun. Then we turn and we are traveling from the South door to the West door. Right before the West door, there are racks on the ground made out of chokecherry branches and those racks are where we turn over our sacred *Cannumpas*, our pipes. The pipe stem is leaning against the rack, the pipe bowl is on the ground but there is sage that is between the pipe bowl and Mother Earth. The sage is placed there because these pipes are sacred. So everybody turns their pipe over to an intercessor. I've done this many times. I would accept the pipe and put it on the rack and then once you have done that you go out the West door into the rest area that is designated for the Sun Dancers.

In the Sun Dance there could be as little as one dancer, all the way up to two or three hundred dancers, so they vary in size. You've got some Sun Dances that are just a family Sun Dance. Members of one *tiwahay* (family) or *tiospaye* (extended family) are invited there. Or a Sun Dance could be open to the tribe. There are a few that do allow non-Indians to participate. That's always a controversy but it is up to the Medicine Man, the spiritual leader to make that call. Sometimes he makes the call but some people will complain about people who are non-Indian. I've seen it where some White people have Sun Danced, and a person that was probably half Indian half Black. One guy from Japan, he was allowed to dance, he would fly in every year from Japan and I'm just talking about up there at the International Sun Dance. But there are other Sun Dances that probably had people from all over the world. There are different viewpoints on this, so it is something that is somewhat controversial. In a way, it depends on how much you want to make it controversial.

Each round of the Sun Dance could last a half hour it could be an hour or it could be longer. When we'd get done we'd go back out the West door to take a break. It could be a half hour or it could be an hour break, then we go back out and dance. You should get in seven rounds at a minimum each day. It's a sacred seven for a sacred number plus the number of our seven sacred ceremonies, seven directions and seven council fires. We try to do seven to be safe and yet you could do more rounds than that. At the end of each round an intercessor will pick up some pipes from the racks and present them to the dancers that own that pipe and those dancers will walk those pipes to the South door. Then the supporters who are out there, who are usually family members or people from that community will stand in front of the South entrance to the altar to accept a pipe.

The South door is where we make the exchange of our pipes that are loaded with our prayers. We present them to the supporters, motioning four times with both hands, reaching out and back with the *Cannumpa*. The receiver also has their hands out and they also motion four times putting their hands out and then bringing them back four times. It is out of respect for this *cannumpa* as a sacred object that we're going to do this motion four times. There is quite a bit of meaning with that motion. The person has four times to think about accepting this Sacred Pipe and if nothing else it makes them think about these ways. It gives them that time to think about accepting the pipe. If you have your hands out there for the fourth time, then the Sun Dancer will place the pipe into your hands. When you accept the red pipestone bowl should be in your left hand, the hand that is closest to your heart. The stem will be in your right hand. It is presented that way. The person who accepts it takes on the responsibility of lighting and smoking that pipe and to take care of it. It's kind of like handing over something sacred, but also like somebody that would hand you a child, a baby. You hold onto it, you care for it; you take precautions, you watch what you say and watch what you do. You have something sacred in your hands and that's the way we are supposed to think all the time, that we have this in our hand. This is a reminder to visualize the pipe in your hand at all times not just during the Sun Dance. Try not to gossip or cuss or fight or drink or do things like that. Try communicating with people so that those good words will come from you, from good thoughts will come good energy.

Late one evening I asked my father-in-law how the Sun Dance was going. He said right when we all entered the East gate on the opening day, there were White Buffalo tracks that were leading him around the bowery. They would just appear in front of him and he was just following this White Buffalo, a Spirit buffalo. He could see the tracks and probably anybody else who was a Medicine Man could probably see it or have that ability to see those kinds of things. Sometimes us common people can see these things, every now and then when they want to show us a sign like this. It kind of reinforces your belief system or your faith in this way of life. But these are all reinforcements to the legend of the White Buffalo Calf Maiden; she came and brought us the Sacred Pipe. Events like this reinforce that and there are many of these sacred events that take place. It could be just for a few seconds or minutes, but they do happen. That's just one of the stories that I have.

I'm gonna talk about another Sun Dance year. I remember that it was really hot out. At the International Sun Dance the two main spiritual leaders were the father-in-law, Sidney Keith and then his adopted spiritual brother Chief Frank Fools Crow, an Oglala Sioux. Franks kind of official title was he was the last of the traditional chiefs or Medicine Men. He was pretty much up there in age, somewhere between 75 and 85 years of age when this took place. My father-in-law, he sat by the South door where the drum group is, where the dancers pass the sacred pipe to the supporters throughout the ceremony. Frank Fools Crow sat to the left of the West door. My father-in-law that day said if you really want to learn something watch Frank Fools Crow, just don't stare at him but keep your eyes on him. 'Cause you had to keep an eye on him as the intercessor for what's going on around the bowery or with the dancers. Some of them might need help. Sometimes you might see a sacred sign, eagles or some type of an animal or something going on, so I couldn't really rest. Some people take little naps during the breaks; as a dancer you can do that because you are expending a lot of energy out there. As an intercessor you have to be aware of what's going on. With my father-in-law being 60 or 70 feet away, we are not talking to each other, but its all body language so we have to watch for these signals.

This one Sun Dance about 10 in the morning I was looking at Frank Fools Crow and he was sitting in a chair not too far from me, maybe about 20 feet. On that particular morning I was looking over there and I seen Frank Fools Crow all of a sudden he turned his head real sharp. He always wore this huge cowboy hat and he turned and he looked in the direction of my father-in-law. So I followed his eyes that way and I seen my father-in-law who was facing towards the East and he looked just a second after that. He looked over and they kind of looked at each other for a while with no sign language or anything, but I felt there was something going on there. Shortly after that Fools Crow called over Vine King and then Vine left the bowery. About 15 minutes later, I could see Vine in Fools Crows camp and I could see him putting some things away and about an hour later he pulled down his tipi. Then I noticed that my father-in-law called his wife over and they were talking for a little bit and then she went back to the camp. She was in charge of the cook shack for the visitors and supporters and she actually took down a tent that was over there.

The sun was out, pure blue sky and from where we are in Green Grass at the International Sundance, you could look to the West and I say you could look for hundreds of miles at the sky and it was pure blue sky all the way.

Each round we take so many pipes or what we call *Cannumpas* or *Cannumpa Wakan* (Sacred Pipes), to share with the supporters. Up until that time we were doing four pipes a round so that if we did ten rounds that would be forty pipes. Sometimes we would take six pipes, depending on how many dancers we had. I noticed that the father-in-law would put up his hand to the intercessors and he would put up at least four fingers for four pipes. Pretty soon he was putting up both hands and I think we started off with eight and then gradually as the day went on we went up to ten. Going on at that pace it looked like we would be over about 3 or 4 o'clock and that is early compared to like 7 o'clock or 8 o'clock.

That afternoon about 3 o'clock, I looked to the west and this is 6 hours after I watched Fools Crow look at my father-in-law. Some really black, dark clouds were coming from the west and within one hour this really bad storm hit. It pretty much knocked over all the tents, took off all that shade we had over the bowery and just disrupted the whole camp. Debris was flying all around. People ran for cover. The Sun Dancers had to stay within their confined area, so we all covered up but everybody was just soaked. It was a very fast hard hitting storm. It probably took about an hour and a half to get things back to normal. We did end the Sun Dance that day on schedule, but the reason why is that we doubled up on the sacred pipes through the rounds, anticipating that storm.

Later on I talked to my father-in-law. Storms like this happen for a reason and I was kind of hinting around about what went on and he said, "Well, this West direction even though it is a Sun Dance, you have to respect that. You pray to that direction for it is a very powerful direction. Thunder Beings that come from there can cause chaos. It's usually good after they leave but they can cause some damage, scare people. People can have accidents and so forth because there is wind, there is rain, there's hail. There is lightning and darkness that comes with that."

He explained what happened, and this is where only a Medicine Man would know this, or could participate in this. I know what happened but I don't know the experience of it, the feeling of it. He explained *there was a vibration that came through Mother Earth, and it hit their feet.* This vibration that came through there and hit their feet, it hit both of them at the same time. When Fools Crow quickly looked over at to my father-in-law and he quickly looked back, they both knew there was going to be a storm even though it was clear blue skies. They knew this was going to happen and they took precautions and they anticipated that this would come. I don't know if it was the intensity of the vibration, maybe it got more intense over time. But there is a signal that is given when things like this are going to happen and they both recognized it and anticipated that there was going to be a disruption in the Sun Dance.

It doesn't ruin the Sun Dance the storm, but it's a teaching tool for some of the rules that go with the Sun Dance that pertain to this West direction. People can have water if it's in their camp and they are allowed to have that. We just don't allow people to bring water or liquids up to the bowery. We do this out of respect for the dancers who can't have any. Even if they are washing dishes or if they can't drink all of their coffee, they take the water that's in the container and lower it to Mother Earth and pour it right on Mother Earth. In other words they are not standing up and they are not throwing water onto the ground. It's one of the rules that have been handed down and there are things that you shouldn't do at a Sun Dance, ***it'll bring on water***.

Another one is washing your hair at a Sun Dance and I have seen this happen where a lady not knowing was washing her hair. I mean if you know these rules you won't break them because you are involved as a dancer so you want to make sure that everything goes smooth. But as a person you can't wash your hair at a Sun Dance. If you are a supporter you can leave the Sun Dance and go to a motel or go to a relative's home or somewhere and you can clean up there. You just can't do it when the ceremony is actually going on at the grounds.

Another one is the idea of bringing in fish, there is a river close by and kids go down there and fish. They do not want you to bring any animal that would want water or depends on water. It could be a fish or a frog, I've seen several people bring turtles and right away somebody recognized that and said you must take those turtles back down to the water, they can't be in the camp during this sacred ceremony. One time we had a turtle shell that had paint in there. We was gonna paint the bottom half of the Sun Dance tree and the father-in-law said, "No. No. No. You can't use that shell". So it doesn't have to be alive, it can be a symbol. But that was part of that animal that shell, so we can't use it, if we did it might have brought rain and we are not trying to make it rain at any Sun Dance.

Another rule is women can't be there during their moon or during their time. It's just that it's a sacred time for the women and it always has been. But they are not allowed there at the Sun Dance. They can camp and would have to be some distance away. I mean maybe like a quarter mile or more and again these rules have been tested or developed hundreds, thousands of years ago. Same way with women in her time she can't be around a sacred pipe. It's nothing bad on their part but it's just the rules that are set up at this time. Mostly all the women know this, even as a young child they have seen this. Some men that have their pipes at their house will ask their woman to stay with a relative until she is done with her time. Some cases I've seen where they've got them a motel room for four days until their time was over. Or you could remove your sacred pipe and put it into a safe place, some places have like a shed or a garage and they can store it there. Most times they would wrap it up in sage, deer hide or some other kind of hide and keep it in a safe place.

As we go through this there are a lot of rules; no cameras, no cell phones-because they could take pictures of the Sun Dance. Nobody can be doing this and people have taken pictures. Some brought in tape recorders, they wanted to tape the music for whatever reason and they have tried to bring back some memory as far as recording something and that is not allowed. No firearms; that is not allowed of course. No alcohol or drugs are allowed at the Sun Dance. Some of the other rules are the women can't wear cutoffs or shorts at these ceremonies. If they have pants on or even if they did have the shorts on they can cover that up with a shawl or blanket or a skirt that goes below their knee. But the most widely used is some of those long kinds of calico dresses (old time dresses I call them) for the women. The men should wear long pants also. There is something of a dress code on this.

Behavior is a big thing, no arguments and especially with children, you can't spank your children and you can't yell at them at a Sun Dance. Its better that you don't tell your children that, but you have to practice it so there's a lot of patience in the Sun Dance as far as some of the kids kind of just running around or misbehaving. They are just basically playing, but you can't yell at them. Again you can talk to them softly and try to convince them to behave in a better way. You could say, "You are at a Sun Dance. This is sacred so behave." It's better to do this throughout the year in teaching them. You can teach them by going to other ceremonies like the *inipi* (the sweatlodge) or to sacred places like Bear Butte or *Paha Sapa* the Black Hills. You can be teaching them throughout the year so that this does not become an issue when they get to the Sun Dance. I've seen it where people do get mad at their kids and then by you getting mad at your kids somebody else would have to come over and talk to you about that behavior so both of you would not feel good about that. I've seen adults argue with each other. One might even leave if their feelings have been hurt. Or if they can't restrain from arguing with somebody else, they might even be asked to leave. There are a lot of rules; most of them are pretty easy to deal with. It's been going on for hundreds of years, anybody can sit down with somebody new that's coming and just go over these rules, take ten minutes to go over with them and everything should be good.

When the ceremony was over for the day, Sun Dancers at the International Sundance had the option of staying within the confines of the Sun Dance grounds or they could go back to their camp, which is kind of a real tempting. You know you have to be pretty strong to go outside of that sacred altar that we have for the Sun Dance 'cause a lot of them made commitments not to drink or eat, so there is a lot of temptation out there. You see water, you see food, you know, anything can happen; somebody could get in an argument with you. You definitely have to be strong and it is somewhat easy to be that way for one or two days. The third day is probably the day that is kind of the hump day that you realize that you only have one day after that. So it makes it kind of tough on you that you are given that freedom to do go back to camp. As intercessors we can go back to the camp, no problem.

A lot of Sun Dances go a half day or two thirds of the day on the last day to allow the Sun Dancers and their families to get together. People have giveaways and feasts for the Sun Dancers. It gives people time to take down their tents before they head out and go traveling back home before it gets too dark.

I do want to mention another time after a day of Sun Dancing, Fools Crow and the father-in-law were sitting around the campfire and I went over there like I usually do at night. Maybe there's another intercessor or two that might come over there and we all kind of pick our time if we want to ask them questions or spend some time smoking a cigarette or visiting. Well I went over there and Fools Crow and Sidney of course they are all speaking fluent Lakota. They were speaking and while I was there listening to them I was trying to figure out about some words and things.

Fools Crow was pointing at his wrist and put his hand up by his head, by his ear. They were talking and my father-in-law he shook his head no and he told him *pilama* or thank you though. So they said goodbye, they had been talking for a good hour or so. I usually asked my father-in-law, "Is there anything I should know about what went on today?" Or, "Can we do anything different tomorrow?" But that night I said, "I'm just curious about what Fools Crow was talking about." He said, "Well he has these stones, round stones and he has them under his skin. He was asking me if I wanted these stones."

Fools Crow had seven small stones under his skin, given to him during a vision. These little stones, there were seven of them. He was also explaining he has some stones behind his ear, either one or both of them. The ones behind his ear were basically a protective type of thing. Also he could probably communicate with a certain spirit, but it was protection against things that were coming up behind him or maybe people talking about him behind his back. I don't fully understand all of it but I know that it was all good. The one in his wrist, if you watched Fools Crow, especially when he addressed the people, he would put his left hand up in the air. Before he prayed he would bring his left hand up in the air and that had something to do with that prayer. Maybe it was for some type of help calling the Spirits or he was told to do this or things would work out more positive or maybe he got the attention of the people this way. He used that in a good way to address the people or address the Spirits. I'm not sure why my father-in-law didn't accept that help or that gift but he didn't accept it. He actually said, "I should have asked Fools Crow if *you* could have those stones." Of course I was excited about that. He said 'Well, he probably has to ask you if you want it but he did ask me and I said not right now, I'm ok." So I remember that conversation we had.

    I remember me, my wife and a couple of my kids were heading from Green Grass into Eagle Butte during the daytime. It was probably a day before the Sun Dance started. We would usually go there like on a Friday or maybe a whole week before the Sun Dance and help prepare the Sun Dance grounds getting things ready. It did take a lot. We had to have some pickups there and hopefully about ten workers there. There are a lot of repairs to make to some things that are worn out from the previous year.

We have to prepare the Sun Dance for the people that are coming there. So right before the Sun Dance started we were going back to Eagle Butte. Off to my left side, between a couple hills, I happened to look real quick and I seen a Chief with a double trail war bonnet eagle feather headdress on a horse. He was where you wouldn't be able to see it unless you were driving and you happened to look. It was right between these two small hills. I looked and I seen this Chief! I thought I was seeing something! As soon as I looked to the wife to have her look over there, of course, we drove a little bit, just a little bit further and it was gone. I looked back and it wasn't there. I mentioned it to maybe two people, 'cause my Father in law was not out there yet. We went into Eagle Butte and then we came back out to Green Grass. When he did come out, either that night or the next morning, I told him about it. He said there have been people who have seen this Chief. The spirit of this Chief watches over this community. He rides all around this area and watches and tries to protect, especially the children and the elders. That's what a Chief does. The strange thing about this was that it was during the daytime. Most things that I have seen have been during the night time but this was right in the day time. I'm not sure what the Chiefs name is. Somebody probably does know on that. So I imagine that this is the same thing that goes on in a lot of Indian communities is that a chief or Medicine Man or an elder and it could even be children Spirits that would watch over, still, their families. They choose to do that.

One time at the Sun Dance, I was speaking with my Father in law, he was telling me about a woman out there dancing. He told me what kind of shawl she had on. He said, "There's a bird that came off the sacred tree, a spirit bird and it flew and it went into this woman. It must have been a good prayer. I could see it but I don't think the woman seen it." So he described the bird to me.

The next day we started dancing and he said, go look at the woman. I looked at her and most of these women have like a pleated skirt and then they would have a shawl on their waist and the fringes might go all the way to the ground or at least to about the ankle. Here the bird that he described the day before, this bird, the color, everything, was the design on the front of her shawl. She wore that shawl the next day that had the symbol, the shape of the bird that flew off the tree. She had some kind of connection to this bird. It was a blessing. It seemed small in a way, but this is something that took place in a sacred way. The one who it's happening to or the Medicine Man or someone who has a connection to this might be the only ones that actually see all the things going on out in the circle.

    I remember one person, a close friend, his father had passed away. When we got done dancing we came back in and he was sitting there and he said, "I couldn't believe it. I looked next to me and my father was dancing. He was Sun Dancing next to me." And his father had never participated in a Sun Dance. He said, "I almost broke down and cried when I seen that. But I felt good that he was there supporting me and my brother and the rest of the Sun Dancers."

    This happened at the International Sun Dance and it came to me in a dream. At the Sun Dance I was like most people; they do their piercing from the chest rope to the tree. You are connected to the sacred tree. Some people have a rope that's connected to buffalo skulls and then that's connected to the back of their body with the skewers. There's a few other ways you can pierce: by hanging from a tree or on a horse, I've seen a horse pierce a lot of people. There are different methods and you can use a combination of these also. A lot of this comes through a dream or vision or through a ceremony if you ask for this or the Spirits might just show it to you. But in my case, of all the years I've sun danced or was an intercessor, I've dragged skulls. And I've only pierced in the front, I'm gonna say maybe only four times. The reason why is because this bowery has the different doors or gates and this east gate is the gate that has the most emphasis during this ceremony. It's where the sun is coming up in the east and it starts to shine through this gate to the tree and then we're going to welcome the sun through prayers and songs.

The dream I had was I was lying at the east entrance and it was either real early in the morning or real late at night. It was dark but there was a hint of light in the sky. There was some real tall grass, like three feet high. I heard something go by me and I was laying not right there in the doorway but off to the side. I heard some singing and I woke up and I was looking through the grass. I could see some feet and then all of a sudden I seen a buffalo skull go by and it was dragging, it was moving through the grass. So I was just watching that, wondering: What's going on here? Well eventually as it passed by I looked up higher and I was at this Sun Dance. On this tree there was maybe fifteen Sun Dancers or so hooked up to the tree. Some were just dancing on their own and then some were dragging the buffalo skulls behind them. They were kind of doing their own thing. Today there is an order that we follow, it's not all individuals going in different directions, but this was. So it looked like it was a long time ago and maybe that's the way they did it. So then I took that dream into a ceremony and they said: since the Sun Dancer was at the east gate and that is where the sun and the buffalo (they are related) conduct the ceremony from, they're showing you that dragging these skulls is what they want you to do. So I went ahead and kept that dream and I really haven't had a dream other than that since then. So, that's my choice to drag the buffalo skulls. While other people might have a dream of how they pierce or what they wear when they pierce; some are painted, some wear certain feathers. I mean there's a reason, how they look, how they act, what they do out there, because of a dream or vision or a ceremony.

When Sidney and his committee brought the Sun Dance back to Cheyenne

River in 1970 there was only one other one that I know of. That was put on by the traditional Medicine Man Frank Fools Crow down in Pine Ridge. He brought back the Sun Dance down there. It had been illegal for a long time, probably since Wounded Knee in 1890. There were actually some people that practiced it after that but the government suppressed and made it a federal policy that the religious ceremonies, especially the Ghost Dance and the Sun Dance cease. They just deemed it to be something that wasn't healthy or civilized.

There are many positive aspects of restoring the ceremonies and it's one of the things that Sidney saw for himself, I'm sure of it. The impact that those huge ceremonies have on a community is very positive. Some of the people that were intercessors or were helpers at those Pow Wows took the Sun Dance concept, how it was run and took it back to their communities and started Sun Dances there. Sidney would invite Fools Crow up too as an advisor and then he would advise how this should be run and then he eventually became a spiritual supporter. He would always be there to ensure that we carry on the ceremony the best we could.

Eleven - Sidney Keith
Stones and Spirits

In the beginning we didn't know anything about Jesus. But Indians knew that we were all related, animals, anything that's alive, all related. Therefore with all beings and all things we are as relatives; that's the way it's supposed to be. No man is supposed to be above the animals so the Indian is humble himself, because all the wild animals are related. They're related to the yellow people and the black people and the white people all related. They told us that we gotta live in this country, work together, but somewhere or another, the technical stuff has got ahead of one man, the white man. He's destroying everything that was supposed to be the way the Great Spirit taught the Indian when they brought this Sacred Pipe. It's a powerful thing, this Pipe is really powerful. Even Fools Crow is scared with it. He cries when he prays and that's the way it's supposed to be. Nobody handles it except the Keeper. I mean, you can touch it and pray while you can touch it. When you go in where they lay that bundle out, you go in and pray, why, it hits you, chokes you up, makes you feel the presence of somebody watching you from up there. So it's a really powerful religion. Nobody knows it and we don't care. It's ours so far. The secret is with the Indians. They got the power, every one of them Indians got the power, but they don't know it. If they want it, like I did, I wanted it, so they gave it to me, because I humble myself. I try to live right. Once in a while, I get mad but that's permissible.

There are five sacred ceremonies that come with the Pipe, we're only doing the *Inikagapi*, that's the sweat lodge pipe ceremony and we did that sacred feast and the Sun Dance. One more, I don't know nothing about it, otherwise I would try it and that's the Saving of the Souls. It's where the cut hair of all your little loved ones, put 'em in that rawhide thing and there's a ceremony that goes with it. You keep it in your house or teepee and if they die, those Spirits are supposed to help them. They'll come to you. They talk to you.

And I saw that, a lot of that happens. You know (name omitted)? One of his kids was playing outside; they didn't have no ball, so they were throwing rocks at each other, catching them. This one girl caught something and looked at it and it was a little bitty rock, round as you could find. She put it in her pocket and started playing. Well, a week later this Grandfather Spirit kept coming through the walls so they're scared to death then! They wanted to know what that meant and they came and asked me. So I questioned them. What happened? What happened to start this thing? And that's when I found out that they were playing with rocks. She said, "Mom, I found that little rock. Remember?" And so she asked, "What'd you do with it?" She said, "It's still in the house."

That's the sacred stone that she got, you see? They should have put it in that little bag and kept it in a safe place, well they didn't know anything about the culture. They lost it, you see. So I told 'em what to do, put it in a bag and put it up on a window sill and pray that you won't see him again. He's trying to tell you something. You don't need him, you're gonna have trouble, you're gonna get yourself in trouble.

I got one of those stones; two years ago it came to the center pole. What happened was unbelievable. When I was standing there, during the Sun Dance, I could feel it, the presence of the Spirits. I sang with them, I knew all the songs and then I thought this would be a good time to ask for something. I wanted to be a Medicine Man some day and that's the way I prayed. I prayed to them that, if I'm qualified, if I'm good enough, spiritually at least, I'd like to have something to get me started.

I prayed for good health and nothing else, good health for my fee. I don't want no money, no riches or nothing. Maybe rich in spirit, you know. But the Spirits don't like that when you ask for something to make you rich. If you use alcohol, they don't like that. It doesn't mix with the Spirits at all, because they're working for the Great Spirit. The Great Spirit is over all these other Spirits, where they are the intercessors to the Great Spirit and the Spotted Eagle.

So I was standing there and I told the Spotted Eagle to give me something, if it's a stone, I want it, so I could start. It went on and on and I just forgot about it. But I kept looking at that sacred pole; they always have to watch that. There's a man and a buffalo, cut out of rawhide, they're hanging there and when you're watching the Sun Dance, you're supposed to watch them. They do action, they dance too and do various things and that's where you can translate a vision from them. So I was trying to look at that and I seen Fools Crow, he has a long feather fan, he's going like this, waving the fan. He was standing facing my way. He was trying to look at something. I was trying to see if that was what he was looking at, those figures.

Pretty soon he went and he grabbed one of those prayer ties, there was a bunch of cloth in all six colors and he signaled like that, you know. "It's okay, I'm going down there." He grabbed something he looked at it and he started dancing around then. They were, at the time they were all standing in a row, in a half-circle. They were all dancing towards the center. So each one, he showed it to 'em. So these dancers, they look at it and then they stand there, next to him. When he got through he showed it to the other guy that was helping him. He tore a piece of that black cloth that was hanging there, 'bout yeh square and he put it in there and tied it up. When he was coming through the two white flags to get out, the way they always get out, I knew he was coming to where I was, so I knew that. Sure enough, he comes towards me! He presented it to me, he said, "Take care of it. He's gonna take care of you. Whatever you want him to do, he'll help." So I got that and I keep it in my little pouch with sage in it. I got it up in my kitchen, top shelf; nobody gets near that one shelf there. That's mine; I put all my stuff there. And sometimes like if I go home late at night and for some reason I open that shelf, I see a blue light, lightning, real fast. So he's there.

Every Medicine Man, when you go up on the hill, the songs come to you, either that or you know some songs. The Spirits can change the words around to suit you, because you all don't get the same Spirit. There's a lot of them up there, waiting. The sacred stones or even the sacred Spirits, those are the ones that talk to you. So when I go on the hill, that's the Spirit I wanna go talk to. I don't know what he is. He might be a deer or an eagle, or woodpecker, owl, whatever. He's the one that's gonna talk to me.

I talked to a different Medicine Man, "Is there a way I can talk to him?" He said, "Yes." I went back to Fools Crow and asked him. He said, "Okay, all you do is go up on the hill, put a little sage, kinda make it like a little nest, take your red stone out and put it on top. Take your pipe and pray to the west, north, east, south winds all six directions." Well before that I have to go through a sweat lodge, purify myself before I can get up there. So I did that down there, by golly, if I didn't! He prayed at the same hour I was going to stand up there and he was gonna pray that this stone was gonna talk to me. Sure enough, first thing, he did it. Something was tapping me on the back. I didn't wanna look back. I stood my ground and pretty soon, "sh-sh-sh", right in my ear. So I took that pipe and I faced it towards him and right away he started talking.

So I still owe him a vision quest. I'm taking it slow, because when I do get it, I wanna get the power. Not to use it against anybody, but I want the power to know more. That's the ultimate in religion. I want to know all that, so I can teach it. So that's the reason I got that stone, because I want to be up on the hill and learn all that, see all the things that you are supposed to see, like Black Elk said. That's the way to do it. You gotta be brave, when you go up there, because you're all alone up there, nobody to talk to except the Spirits. If you're qualified, if you're good enough, if you're Indian, they'll come to you. You just sing a song or two, sacred songs, that is. I know all of them. So that's the way you get your power.

There's a lot to this thing, but I'm just scraping the top. Some of the older people knew all about it, but they kept it to themselves, because they don't believe in writing anything down. They didn't even know how to write it down. Now you do, you've got tape recorders, movies, things like this, but still the Spirits won't perform in front of the television or a camera. Or they might. I heard it on a recording! They recorded songs! I could hear that rattle in there! They can do that and they like to show up, that they're in there. I've got some at home that you can hear those rattles in their songs. But the Medicine Man is not the one that's doing it. That's why *yuwipi*, they tie their hands behind their back, they're laying there all tied up, but you can't go in there and unhook him yourself. You gotta let the Spirits do it. They do it fast too! They even roll up those tobacco offerings. They're all hooked together, four hundred and some, they're rolled up in real nice balls. Real fast! They take those flags down and lay 'em down where that little altar is there where he makes his designs. And the designs that he made, they're really messed up. Sometimes you see deer tracks, trampled all over. They're good; they're the professionals, these *yuwipi* men. So if I was a Medicine Man, you know, I'd stand up and do my thing and they'd come. But if I want to be a real professional, I can be a *yuwipi*, let them take me.

    I'll tell you a good one from before this Medicine Man Blue Hair got killed on the highway. What he did was, down in Cherry Creek one time he was gonna have an *inikagapi* but somehow they didn't get the firewood and stuff ready. So we just let it go, we figured we'd go home and we was gonna come back late at night. So I stopped at his house and here he came over and said, "I'm not gonna let it go so easy. Are you going home now?" I said, "Yea." He said, "Can I go home with you?" I said, "Why?" I mean, he lived right there. He said, "I want to show you something. You take me to Eagle Butte and you know where that railroad track is? Dump me off there. When you dump me off, you go back to your house and call me here at Cherry Creek and I'll answer you from here."

    He was betting everybody, well, he wasn't betting them, but he said he could do it! And these people say, "No! No! No!" They were afraid of him that he can do it! They believe in him that much. Well nobody wanted to do that, at least I didn't! I don't want to see him do it! But he knows that the Spirits can take him over there, that quick. He believes in it that much that they can do it and they did it! All the other people heard him say that, they said, "No! No! No! Who's gonna call him?" but they did one time and he did what he said he could do. He did it! I'm scared of them!

Twelve - Melvin Miner
The Mark on the Forehead

I remember a visitor came over to my father-in-law's house. He presented a pipe or a cigarette. He was talking to my father-in-law and I was just over there visiting myself, so I kind of sat in on part of the conversation. Sometimes you can listen in and sometimes you have to kind of walk away and let them talk. So I went in the living room and sat. They got done and this person was a pretty good friend of mine. I went in there after he left. I'm not sure what the problem was. I was sitting there and my father-in-law said, "Did this person have a drug problem at one time?" I said, "Yeah. I believe there were a lot of drugs. Can you tell when somebody has this problem?" He said, "Yes. For me there is a black stripe across the forehead. It's small. So this I know is contributing to whatever problem that they have. Tells me something about what went on with this person." So that was a visible sign that tells him. Maybe that's not true with other medicine men. I'm not sure, but it was something that was interesting to know. But it was one of the clues for him, other than the Spirits talking to him, of finding something out about an individual.

I remember one day everybody got up early. Sidney and his wife were living with us and we got up and it was early, probably like 6:30 or 7am. Sometimes that's really early for us 'cause I'd usually stay up doing arts and crafts, until 12 or 1 o'clock. It was nice and quiet then; I could concentrate better without a lot of activities going on in the daytime. I got up and seen coffee was made so I sat down and he was sitting there. He was smoking a cigarette and he said, "Something sad is going to happen today. I had a dream and in this dream this lady from the west was crying." So I prayed at that moment. Shortly after he told me this, we received a phone call. A lady on the other end was crying. She said that somebody passed away through the early morning. She wanted some prayers for this person and to see what Sidney could do. " That's what I was afraid of." he said," I was going to get a call or someone was going to come over, so I got up early, but I prayed for this situation, for the family and for this woman. I don't like it when I hear somebody crying at night time. I know somebody passed away." So the dreams that come to him, he actually heard this crying through the night.

Another time I went over to his house; he lived in Rapid then. I went over and we were having coffee. My wife was usually talking to her mother. Sidney was still laying down, he wasn't sleeping, he was kind of resting. He was up throughout the night. So the mother was talking to Sandy and she said, "I never get used to this, but Spirits, they come at 3 o'clock in the morning, when it's dark and they talk to him. So he gets up and sits on the edge of the bed. And he's speaking Lakota to them. I can hear them speaking to him and sometimes they'll speak for a long time, but it keeps me up. I'm kind of listening, but at the same time I'm kind of scared. So anyhow he stayed up and he talked to them and sometimes its hard for him to go back to sleep. He never tells me what they are telling him. He just, I ask him and he's like, 'Oh, I don't know. They're just talking to me.' But they come all the time. He's not scared; he just talks to them like he talks to anybody else." "So," she said, "He's kind of tired from staying up. So Sandy and I were kind of looking at each other and said, "Okay, well, we'll come back later."

One time while we were there at the house the father-in-law sat in there close to the coffee pot, then I would usually sit across from him. He would be really quiet and he wouldn't look at you. He would be thinking. He could be quiet for hours and hours. I remember one time he said:

I'm not trying to be rude or nothing, but people say things. This is sacred when we speak and you could say the wrong things and hurt somebody's feelings. The voice has a lot of power. Both ways, you could speak peace and love or good things. But you can also speak and get angered. You could cuss or you could cause a lot of pain that way. But if you notice when I'm spoken to, I speak, but I practice silence, just meditating. If the Spirits talk to me when I'm like this they help me. They tell me what's gonna happen, not all the time, but a lot of times.

We were there and he'd pretty much be like this. You know we'd have a lot of visitors come over. He would speak to them and drink coffee. He smoked some and he always advised people not to over-smoke and if you do then maybe you should smoke your *cannumpa* more.

I remember one night in the kitchen, probably about 10 o'clock at night and the father-in-law was sitting in the kitchen. "Did anyone make a promise to make some tobacco ties?" I know both my wife and me both looked at each other and said "No, I don't think so." He said, "Well, there's four Spirits outside. They are old men and they usually come looking for these tobacco ties that are promised to them. There's one in the car. There's one looking up the tree. There's one on top of the house on the roof and there's one looking around the yard. The prayer ties are not outside." Just then his wife, the mother-in-law, said, "I did make a promise to make some tobacco ties. He said "Whoa. When was this?" She said, "Like about six days ago." He said, "Whoa. You know that you are supposed to make them when you promise. You are supposed to make them within *four days* of your promise. Well. What did you promise?" She said, "Well, I was coming back from Eagle Butte and there was a thunderstorm. I was by Newell up by Bear Butte. You know I'm scared of lightning." So she was in the car in the thunder and she said, "If you just get me through this, I'll make some tobacco ties." So anyhow she didn't do it. And she said, "Oh, I feel so bad." He said, "Well, they're here. I'm gonna tell you something. All of you. If you say you are going to make something, especially tobacco ties and you don't do it then things are gonna come back on you. Times are a little bit tough, they don't want to come back on you but they're going to. You can't make promises and not keep them." So he told her, "You make those 75 prayer ties right now, plus you make some more. And then you put out some food and something to drink for them. You ask them too that you made a mistake and ask for forgiveness. That you learned a lesson and that you won't do this again 'cause you want to be in their favor. You don't want them to get mad at you or not believe you, because they are there to help you."

So we helped her. She made the ties and we put out some food and things. I think she might have sung a song. Things worked out. Some people don't believe that Spirits come for these offerings, but they do come and they appreciate that. I know my father- in-law, just from working with him, he put out food. He put out what we call spirit food: *wasna* and chokecherry juice, coffee, cigarettes, tobacco. He would put flags out there, especially our six sacred colors for an offering. These are things you can make for an offering for the Spirits. Then you put prayers with that food, with that chokecherry juice, with that tobacco, with those flags. You put out meat, you put prayer with that and they will come take your prayer through that. So, it does happen and they do come and that night I learned quite a bit and maybe not only one Spirit will come, in that case there were four of them. They came for that one purpose. And again, probably only a Medicine Man or somebody that the Spirits allow is going to be able to see this.

One time we were going down to Phoenix for a crafts show. I remember there was some snow on that trip so I'm guessing it was early winter when we took this trip. We did a lot of traveling back then but we always offered tobacco to the father-in-law and asked for a good trip. He prayed and before we left he said, "The only thing the Spirits say is that they don't want no alcohol or drugs in the vehicle. Everything will be alright." And we didn't use either, so I was wondering about that, why that was mentioned. Well anyhow we headed out. We had to go pick up a relative from Pine Ridge and I think we were going to drive all night. So it was actually pretty late like maybe 9 or 10 o'clock at night. We left

Rapid City and we went down to Pine Ridge and we picked up this relative, I won't mention his name. The relative had a couple of bags and he was going down to Phoenix and to visit while we were down there for about 4 or 5 days.

So we picked up this relative and we started to head south out of Pine Ridge. We were going to go through Nebraska and Colorado and Albuquerque into Flagstaff and into Phoenix. We picked up the passenger and probably about half an hour or forty five minutes into our trip the passenger was driving. He was going to help us out and drive so I was falling asleep, I had a long day. I was in the front seat and here all of a sudden I looked up and it looked like a huge horse was going on to the road. I reached over and touched the guy on the arm and said, "Watch out!" All of a sudden we hit the front end of whatever it was. I didn't know what at the time. It was dark and it just kind of came out of nowhere. So it looked like we hit the front of the animal. We had a station wagon at the time. Well, we went into the ditch. We got out and we couldn't see the animal at all. My wife, who was in the back said it was an elk. The nose of the elk ran all the way along the driver's side windows, all the way to the back and there was a little bit of mucous, a little bit of blood and some other stuff there, it kind of rubbed the full distance. Then the racks of this elk went ahead and tore off our luggage that was on top and that all ended up in the ditch. The radiator was overheating. We weren't too for from town, like maybe a quarter mile and we started the car enough to get out of the ditch. Then it wouldn't run and we had to push it. Some car or truck came along and pushed us into town. The fan made grooves on the radiator so we took off the radiator and sealed it up. We ran some water through there and it wasn't leaking. We put the radiator back on and we headed out.

    The next day, ever what town we were in, Sandy called back to her Dad. Her Dad said, "Did the elk scare you?" She said, "Yes! We hit the elk! We went in the ditch and all of our luggage was torn off!" He said, "Well, ever who you guys picked up had some alcohol or drugs in his bags." Sure enough, we talked to the person and he had a six pack of beer within those bags. We weren't even thinking about that at the time, but the elk was his elk! Sidney's Elk! Like I said, as soon as we stopped we didn't see no animal at all. Sidney knew right away what happened. We kind of paid somewhat of a cost for that mistake. Another thing he did say, "That person is supposed to come back with ya, but that person has a drinking problem. That person is going to end up staying down in Phoenix." So about four days later we packed up early in the morning to head back and that person was there all packed up, had everything, even put his bags in the car. We were saying good bye to my sister Paulette and we started backing out and here this person said, "Hold on! I think I'm just gonna stay in Phoenix." I said, "Oh, okay." So they got his bags out and we headed out and made it back home okay, but everything her Dad told us could happen or would happen did happen.

So it was just kind of another experience. Sometimes if those Spirits are watching you and if you don't follow the rules that are pretty easy to follow then things could happen. I wouldn't say serious things, things that kind of hinder the journey.

Several times this next story has happened. Sidney and Shirley were still living in Eagle Butte and my wife and me were living out in Lakota Homes in Rapid City. I remember we were sleeping and all of a sudden we could hear this flapping noise inside of our room. It woke us up. We could hear it. It was pretty much pitch dark in the room. I could hear a bird flying around inside and the wife woke up and we just listened to it. It flapped around like it was flying around about three, four, five times and it left. The wife called her Dad early in the morning and I was listening. She said, "Dad." Then she stopped and listened. "Yeah, that eagle must have been the bird that came last night." When she got off the phone, she said, "He just said he wanted to check up on us down here, so he sent his eagle down." And that happened a few other times.

I remember one time up in the Black Hills camping. The eagle came to our tent and was flying around inside and then actually sat on the pole right outside the tent. We could see it through the tent, a little bit of the outline of it and then it moved on. So he has done this several times. Also I've been in ceremonies where somebody might have been sick in the hospital and Sidney's Eagle would go to that hospital and then check on that sick person, evaluate that person and in some cases heal that person while he was in the hospital, then would come back and tell him. Then he would tell all of us. He would say, *"Wanbli Gleska* has evaluated this person and this person is going to be alright'" Or he would say, "This person has a serious medical condition and this is what needs to be done." Or he would say, "This is what has to be done.'" So that's pretty normal, not only the eagle but the black-tailed deer, the elk and other Spirits also perform these healings.

Thirteen.-.Sidney Keith
Family History of Medicine People

I have been involved in this thing from when I was a little kid. My dad was a Medicine Man and my step-dad was a Medicine Man. My grandmother, she knew all about it, but she didn't have no power. My mother knows some about it that when somebody's sick, why she goes over there and puts her hand on their head and prays. One time there was a young girl, about fifteen, she was gonna have a baby, way out in the country. Two days earlier they took the girl to the old Agency and the doctor was really mad! "It is impossible to have that baby, because your frame is not big enough to have a baby!" he said. But she did! They came to get my mother. I don't know how this lady knew her, but she couldn't go to nobody that knew anything about child delivery. But she knew that my mother was older and knew maybe if she prayed, something would happen. So they went and got her and she did this same thing. She prayed and put her hands on her head and prayed and sure enough, she had the baby, no sweat! So there again the power of prayer is pretty strong with the Spirits working for you.

My grandfather *Wanbli Wakuwa* Ray Eagle Chaser his name was. He was a good man. He wasn't someone to battle with Custer and stuff like that. He's been through Sun Dancing, he's got a lot of scars on his chest to show that he did that and also wounds that he had. He died when he was 95 years old and I was 6 years old, I think. So 50 years ago he was 95 years old. That's been many years. Before you were even born, you know. He was a policeman for 30 years at Cherry Creek. That's the time that the government provided Indian policeman in each district and he was one. He was there for 30 years. The government paid him. He was also a scout in the Calvary. My mother still has his picture where he's riding a horse with the Army hat on. There's a whole line of Calvary lined up and he's in there. So she's got a picture of him.

My grandfather had three brothers; not the real ones but they were all half brothers, Holy Bull (*Tatanka Wakan*) and Grouse Running (*Siyo Inyanke*) and Brown Dog (*Sunka Gi*) and there is Eagle's Nest (*Wanbli Hopila*), he's an Oglala. He's named after that hill down there, southeast of Wanblee. The butte down there is the Eagles Nest, Wanbli Hohpila. Some other family names were Distribution and Important. My name should be Important. That is who my dad was, he changed it to Important. He used it a lot. One of his grandfathers was laying in a teepee when a bunch of Crows came in and he didn't have nothing but a knife and he really cut them up pretty bad. He used a knife, instead of using a bow and arrow, he used a knife on them. So that's how they called him Uses The Knife. He liked that name, so he thought, "I'll just use that." In those days, you didn't have to stick to a name. Names came just from what they do, Bravery, also Important and so you took that name. But it's a real name! It's still written in Pine Ridge it's 'Important.' If there's a little land allotment check that we get it's signed over in my name now! It would be a small check, maybe two or three dollars! I'm an heir to all that, so that's why those names do appear there. It's a long name and 'Important' and 'Distribution' and 'Uses The Knife' is mine! Keith is a last name that I picked out; it's a better last name, because my art instructor said it was too long to use to sign my paintings

My grandfather made us kids toys. The bow is called *itazipa* and the arrows are *wahinkpe*. These are not the *wahinkpe* that they use for hunting; it's what they call *miyostaka*. It's mainly for kids to play with. They have the blunt end and they're not so powerful. They can hit each other, they'll cry but they won't hurt 'em, unless you get up too close. But they usually shot dogs and stuff or you can kill rabbits with it, if you get up close. The ones I had were made shorter. The heads were short and they had a good, big ball at the end. My grandfather got hit by one, by one of us I suppose, running around playing. He was lying around naked with just a breechcloth (laughing). We shot him in the rear end. He hollered to my grandmother, "*He, miyostake mayelo!*" That's the favorite way of saying, "They shot me!" with that thing the *miyostaka*. So she'd go and chase us around. But *he* made it for us, so. (Laughing- with a gesture indicating the inevitable). We used to play with them. Even when I was a little kid, they still existed.

But the grandfather I had was still pretty smart. He was ninety some years old then and still his mind was really clear. He made things like they used to. And that's why my grandmother made them, he told her to make these things for me. Also, the first son always has to have these things made for him. So, I had to have one of those baby carriers and one of those *cekpa ognake* (umbilical cord bags) and I had to have one of those bow and arrows.

Wanbli Wakuwa (Eagle Chaser) made me everything. He showed me everything. He used to sit us down, a bunch of us boys, tell us stories. He'd use a belt, you know, if somebody's looking the other way. And he used to have a little whip, about that long (indicating height above the floor- four or five feet). He never whips anybody, but that one he uses with the little ones, to scare 'em. When he cracks that why (chuckles) all those kids sit down. But I'm always standing there, or sitting there like this (laughing, gesturing with chin propped on hands and eyes wide open). Ya know? Because I really respect him because he's a storyteller. Not all of the stories are good, but the story had what you could use. It's a story within a story. You can learn it, there's a moral you could use. *Iktomi* stories always have a moral to the story.

They were all good at something. My grandfather, like he was making those pipes and *itazipa* (bows) we were using. He knows how to mix *cansasa* (tobacco) because they've got to mix it some way. Old men would come by and say, "*Cansasa luha hwo*", "Tobacco, do you have some?" He has an extra bag. He'd be sitting all day with a piece of wood and the *mina kaskan*; it's a knife blade like that. (Gesturing. Indicating a curved knife blade). He cuts a bunch of them and they're all really cut good. Then he puts those away in a different bag, it looked like a long muslin bag, he fills that up. Those old guys come and say, "You got any more *cansasa*?" He gives them some. He just gives it away.

After we young boys learned to smoke, about eight or nine you know, he keeps a pouch and he switches it at night. We'd go sneak in there and fill the pipe up and run outside and sit down with it. Light it. The first big puff why we were choked by the smoke. So he was smart. But if you sit there, when you're smoking a pipe, he'd say, "*Han*", (here) you know and give it to you. You'd have to smoke it. He's looking at you, But like this (indicating looking surreptitiously, out of the corner of one's eyes) to make sure you inhale it too. The first time I recall, I gagged on it. After a while, you know how much to inhale it. Chuckling.

Well I think most of the time he was making them for somebody, because I never seen him sell any. He never sells it. He buys something off somebody, or trades with somebody. He doesn't have nobody to trade with him, or buy anything, he gives 'em away. My grandmother used to take care of that. She takes care of all his stuff. He sits down, he'd say," *Cannumpa, mikanbo!*" (My tobacco and pipe!) She'd go and get it, wherever she put it, you know. She's in the house. She don't let any of the kids play with anything of his, we don't play with.

Wasposli patapi (face covering embroidered) is a baby cover, describing a baby cradle. They said they had me in one of those. Now this could be beaded, or all porcupine quills. Those are something to look at! So they said I was, being the first son, which I am, all my grandmothers, there were four of them, they all made them. One was beaded like this and three were all quilled. My grandmother used to use a stove-type salt shaker to smooth them porcupine quills out. When she was finished, then she'd smooth 'em out, kind of irons them. They tried to out do each other, because they'd see who could make the best. So I had one of those things. They used to hang me up on the tree, on a branch.

I know they made one for me, but my brother never did have one. He was born three years after I was. I never heard my mother say that he had one. She tells me that I had four of them. After they named me, on the Fourth of July Celebration, my grandfather was usually up front in the parade. They put me in the best cradle they had and my mother carried it, so they could see me. They'd say, "This little boy's *Naca Cikala* (Little Chief)". That's my name. That's the way they'd do it. I'm her son, the grandfathers were always bragging about her son, the grandson. So that's the way all people know you by that name. They wouldn't say, "Hau, there's Sidney!" They'd say, *"Naca Cikala."*

Quilts were all done by hand. Later, they were issued sewing machines, so my mother used to be pretty good at that at making quilts. I remember watching her make those when I was a kid, all different designs. Star quilts haven't bee around too long, only about the last five years or there about. Before that any kind of design was good, like this one, a cross. But Indians got smarter as they come along. I think the Navajo's down in Oklahoma have got this exploding sun design, which is a star, over here. The real star should be seven pointed, but now, they make 'em any kind of star. That's a good design. I like the star quilts, they're made with different colors and designs.

Owinja paskiskapi means it's quilted. *Paskiska* means "put together" but in different colors. *Ska* is short for, some quilts they put strings in between, you know, to hold it together. *Akicaska* is to sew or baste on, see just like I added that *ska* on the end, because a long time ago, my mother used to make this regular *owinja*, with *akicaska* in between there. Then they learned to make this kind of quilt tops. They just added that little *ska* on there *paskiska. Oqinja* is just a quilt, plain. Then they have this *paskiska* this is made into a kind that's put together like this with small pieces sewn together into patterns and then quilted.

My mother was one of the best *parfleche* painters. She made real difficult designs on there, real difficult. She uses the regular *wase* (red earth paint) the kind you stick in the water with a bone brush. She mixes 'em in bowls, sticks it in there (gesturing as with a brush). She makes the designs, they're really good. Always the same colors, the same kind of design, but they're a little different each time. They're all pretty, she knows how to mix the colors different ways. It doesn't conflict with each other and it's not an eyesore. Look at the design, one color doesn't stand out, they all blend, there's not one to overpower the other. She was really good at it. She makes brown too. I don't know how she does that. She outlines with brown. I've copied that off of her. I don't know if you've seen any of my paintings, the small ones, the acrylic ones? Those up there, (indicating the two large murals, on canvas, hanging in the Cultural Center) I did those in brown, see? Never black. That's what I got from my grandmother, she never uses black. It does something to it, it kills it.

Fourteen - Melvin Miner
A Trip to New York City

Sandy and I went with Charles Fast Horse and his family *tiospaye* to Pittsburg and on to New York City. We had a drum group, the Black Hills Singers and some dancers that went with us. One morning we went to The Museum of Natural History. Sandy and I had a Pinto that the backseat folded down where we had our bedding and suitcases and stuff. We had a few craft pieces but the Fast Horses; it was pretty much a show with them, they had all their arts and crafts and a lot of beadwork. We were in there for maybe a couple of hours before lunchtime. We went outside and saw that our car door was open. We looked in there and anything of value was taken. We had our pipes hidden where the rear seat folds down, where the spare tire would be and even those were stolen in broad daylight. There were about seven or eight construction workers working about 20 feet from there. The construction workers said they did not see anybody inside the car. But we found a screwdriver, there was a screwdriver left inside of our car. They must have used that somehow to pry the door open.

We went back inside the museum and they have security cameras. It so happened that the cameras man for some reason was taking a break so he turned off the cameras. They actually said that this had happened several times and so there was some sort of connection there with the camera man and ever who broke into our car. We went ahead and spoke to Charles Fast Horse about this; we all agreed we should have a sweat. Somebody did have a sweat lodge somewhere in that area and we had a sweat either that night or the next day. The Spirits told him that two young black males stole our pipes and that the image that they showed him was a one of these black males was smoking one of the pipes, using some kind of drugs. They said he's getting sick and so eventually he'll stop doing this and he'll figure out that this is not right, it's not good for him. They said that we're going to have to get new pipes once we get back to South Dakota.

When we came back we had a sweat with Sidney. All we told him was that our pipes had been stolen. Inside the sweat lodge he said the same interpretation. He said two young black males stole these and they were trying to smoke drugs (probably marijuana) inside there but they were getting sick and having bad luck. So they're going to give them away or try to throw them away. He said that we'd need to go ahead and get some new pipes later on. It was good to know they had the same interpretation and this I have seen quite a few times with different Medicine Men. They would almost be the exact interpretation, so wherever they get their information from, their Spirit, it's almost the same.

I'm going to talk about a ceremony that took place out in Lakota Homes. There were some people visiting from out of state. It wasn't in our house; we went to another house that had a basement. We darkened all the windows and he set up his altar and started to sing the calling songs. All of a sudden there was a big flash by this one guy. He was one of the visitors. There were probably about five visitors. There was a big old flash over there and it went on for maybe 15 seconds and it was huge. Not just a little flash but it was huge, probably about six feet by about four feet. You could just see blue and yellow lights. You could see the different colors but it looked like something was clashing. This guy that came, he lived his life in the bars and he drank a lot and that was his lifestyle he said for 20 or 30 years. He brought in a Spirit with him and it was a bad Spirit. When he came into the ceremony the good Spirits actually clashed with this man's bad Spirit that he brought into the ceremony. It's the only time I have ever seen this and there was a struggle going on, because they had to remove this bad Spirit from this man. He obtained this bad Spirit through drinking or he obtained it through the bars. He told us later that he couldn't quit drinking, that this was a major aspect of his life. It was quite an experience to see this thing happen inside there.

One interpretation I heard later on in a sweat lodge was that we all have a good Spirit and when this alcohol came to our people we fed that bad Spirit. We fed it with alcohol, hate, jealousy. That bad Spirit grew bigger in the good Spirit inside of us. It doesn't happen to everybody but to some people and it takes over your mind. If you don't receive Spiritual help then it's going to continue to have you make bad decisions or to walk on this black road. This is the way that we explain how somebody we know is a good person but has drank so much and has allowed that bad Spirit to take over their body. That's why it's so hard for even a Medicine Man to treat people who are drinking because that Spirit won't let that help come in. It's one of the reasons some of our people take so long to heal, because they have to, they don't have to, but its better that they quit drinking and allow the alcohol to be removed from their system. It could take thirty days, it could take longer and that will allow that bad Spirit to be weakened and then we'll have a ceremony and when we pray for this person that a good Spirit will help them. They will have a fighting chance then. If not, if they have only been sober for a few days or a week, that Spirit is still active and that person, chances are will probably fall off the wagon. So we have rules with the Sun Dance or the *hanbleceya* or even picking up a pipe. This might be a modern rule and might be something that's a precaution is that they want you to be sober for one year before you *hanbleceya*, before you do the Sun Dance, before you pick up a pipe. They want you to make sure that you are ready to make this commitment to what we call the Red Road. To be ready to walk this Red Road with the Sacred Pipe or participate in the ceremonies to learn your culture and help people we want you to be sober for a year. So it's a rule that not everybody follows but it's a starting point where people are being told to do this. I've heard this many times and in different ceremonies with different Medicine Men. People who want to participate in something but they're just starting off, so they want to give them time to think about it.

One day I was driving up a hill by where I work at the Sioux Indian Museum. It was daylight and there's this bar. I looked at this bar 'cause there was a woman standing there, long black hair *and I recognized her*. I was wondering, "What's she doing there all dressed up?" Even with a dress on and everything she looked out of place. It looked like she should have belonged in church and I was thinking to myself, "Wow!" This woman was looking straight ahead and then all of a sudden she bowed her head and her hair all went down in front of her. I looked to see where I was driving and I looked back and the she wasn't there. A few days later I was visiting Merle Whistler and I told him about it. I said this was really strange, but this lady was standing in front of this bar and I explained everything to him. He said, "Well it's not that strange, because I also saw this lady, but she was sitting down." He said he was told by a Spirit to pray for her, her Spirit or her soul was caught up in drinking and into the bar scene. The prayer was to pray that she would escape from that life. This person could be a good person; people cared about her, but she needed some prayers. She had been there, been through that for a long time. She wanted to be released from that and we seen the same person, just within a few days on that so we both were told that we have to pray for this person, so we do that.

When Sidney and his wife moved down here from Eagle Butte to Rapid City, we were sweating at a few different places. The whole family developed a relationship with an artist, a sculptor. He does a lot of sculptures in this area and nationwide. His name is Dale Lamphere and he had a place out by Pleasant Valley located on this hill. He allowed us to put a sweat lodge and we sweated and had ceremonies there. Actually several of us did a *hanbleceya*; we fasted up on this hill. It was pretty isolated. He had neighbors but there was a lot of isolation, there was a lot of trees on this hill.

In the mean time Dale wanted to do some sculptures of Indian people in South Dakota. Sandy, my wife was one of them. Some years ago she was chosen as

Cheyenne River Princess so that was a pretty high honor for her. He did a clay mold sculpture and then they bronze it and he actually did this with quite a few different people. Some years later here in Rapid City we went to a bank to cash a check. We were waiting in line and here somebody said, "Sandy!" We were up at the counter to cash the check and she turns around and she says, "What did you want?" I Said, "I didn't say anything." I heard something though and she said, "Boy that really sounded clear." There was a statue there and I said, "Well, maybe the statue said something." We looked at it and it was a statue of her! We really didn't even notice it when we came in and we said, "Hey, look! It's of you!" I guess the statue itself called out her name. I could hear it faintly but she heard it like she thought it was me calling her name. So we looked at it, then we started looking all around the bank and we seen the other statues that Dale Lamphere made. He had a display down there and there were maybe 10 bronze sculptures that were down there so we went around looking at all of them. But something had a voice there; a Spirit within that statue or maybe just a Spirit that wanted us to notice this. The bank must have went ahead and purchased these statues. I went down there in 2008 and the statue was still there with the other ones, but instead of being spread out they were all in one place, kind of a display.

Back in history Sitting Bull was going to travel from his homeland which is Standing Rock Reservation in North Dakota, down to Wounded Knee, but he was killed before he could make that trip. In December of 1890, the Big Foot people (this is Chief Big Foot) from the Minneconjou of the Cheyenne River Sioux tribe made this trip. On December 29th, down in Wounded Knee the Pine Ridge Reservation they had an encounter with the 7th cavalry. Almost 300 of our people were killed, a lot of them women and children. We call it the Wounded Knee Massacre. A lot of people think the 7th cavalry were thinking of revenge for what took place at Greasy Grass or the Battle of Little Big Horn up in Montana.

There's a respected person down in Pine Ridge Reservation named Birgil Kills Straight. He had a dream about a memorial ride, The Big Foot Memorial Ride, retracing their steps starting up where Sitting Bull's people are and coming all the way down to Wounded Knee on horseback. They start the ceremony when they start the trip. They come down and they end the ride with a ceremony called Wiping of the Tears. Relatives of these ones that were massacred are going through a healing process and the men, the warriors retrace these steps.

The memorial ride began in 1986 when a handful of Lakota riders decided to follow the December 1890 trip across South Dakota taken by Chief Big Foot and his followers. That year, Sitting Bull, living on the Standing Rock Sioux Reservation, was killed when resisting arrest by reservation police. After he was killed, Big Foot's band fled Standing Rock and had hoped to spend the winter in safety with the Oglala in the Badlands. They were intercepted and killed by the 7th Cavalry outside Wounded Knee, which sits at the juncture of three creeks on the Pine Ridge Indian Reservation in southwestern South Dakota.

Before they started this ride, I was approached by Birgil Kills Straight to make a ceremonial staff. He had several eagle feathers and we had enough that matched that were from the same bird, so that was probably like 10 or 12. These feathers would go on the staff itself and on the top part, kind of like a cane with a little hoop there. He presented me with these feathers and he explained these were feathers he received from these Medicine Men. I know it was Fools Crow, Big Road, Dawson No Horse and there were a couple other ones, I'm not sure who it was but these Medicine Men all were deceased. I wanted to make sure these were put on the staff. These feathers are sacred in their own right but coming from these Medicine Men has more meaning to it, a blessing. He was saving them and he decided to use them for this. We went out and got the willows and covered the willow with buffalo hide. Then we started to decorate it and put on the eagle feathers. We were smudging the room at the time. Anytime that you work with eagle feathers if you are making something for the Sun Dance or even for a Pow Wow outfit anything like that ceremony, it's good to have the sage and then smudge yourself, the room and the feathers. Of course if a woman is involved, she can't be in her moon at that time or around the eagle feathers.

    Sandy and I were working on that staff and Birgil was going to come and pick it up the next day, I was attaching the eagle feathers. We had a pretty big work table and my wife was sitting across from me doing some beadwork. Her head was down and then she looked up all of a sudden and then she put her head down real quick. I noticed that something was going on and so I said, "What?" She said, "Nothing." So I finished attaching those feathers onto that staff. I remember we were working pretty late that night and so I said, "Well, it'll be good to get it done tonight." Then Birgil would be over sometime in the morning to pick it up. When we got done with it, she said that when she looked up, "I seen four men, Lakota's, standing behind you. I just looked at them and they looked back, so I put my head down. It's not polite to stare. I didn't want to tell you at the time, but my heart was still racing from seeing this." Birgil came the next day and we didn't really know all the details of what was going on with this ride, but he explained it to us. He asked us if he owed us anything and we said no. This was a good honor for us to do this, to make this. We told him what went on with the Spirits in the room, so we know that for sure those Spirits are going to be with this ride. So we shook hands. We learned a lot through that. We know that there are Spirits around; not only the Medicine Men Spirits but we know the animal Spirit, the eagle that we used and also the buffalo, those Spirits can show themselves, especially if it's a sacred thing that we're going to be making.

We make a lot of arts and crafts, sometimes it's sold to tourists, sometimes to a collector, sometimes to a museum, sometimes given away as a gift. But, for sure if we are making something for a ceremony or for a sacred reason we know those Spirits are there so we always do the sage. With that I also made a staff for the Black Hills Pow Wow. I also made a staff for Sidney and he would use it at the Sun Dance and also for some of the more community or social gatherings. Also I made a staff for a gentleman named Paul Wounded Head. People would bring over their own feathers for this. I noticed he uses his staff at the Pow Wow's and in the Grand Entries. Also I made one for the Two Bulls Family. They have an annual Pow Wow they put on in the honor of Nellie Two Bulls. And actually Nellie, even before she passed away she had this annual community Pow Wow down at her place. These staff's are very important and I know that they help out. They're just not there for decoration. They are there and they have a place there and they have a power that ever who is using it or for whatever cause and it helps protect the ceremony for what it represents.

Out in Lakota Homes; there was this guy name of Milo Black Crow. He would come up to the house, I would go down to his house, but we both made arts and crafts. One thing I'm really thankful for, this guy showed me how to make a buffalo headdress in a simple way, yet it looks really nice. I was doing it a much harder way. He helped me with this. But he would have materials, I would have materials and we would trade with each other. He came up to the house and he had these three eagle bone whistles and he gave them to me. He said, "I know you guys go to the Sun Dance. Maybe there's some Sun Dancers who might need these." So I said, "Thanks. I will. I'll give them away."

That same day, the wife said, "Come outside." So I came outside and there were three eagles. One eagle was flying above another eagle above another, going in a circle above the house. I said, "Oh Wow! I got three eagle bone whistles this morning." She said, "Well let's go see my Dad." So we went over there and I gave him tobacco and I told him the story. He said, "There are going to be three people, men that are going to come to your house. You are going to offer these whistles to them because they don't have one. They are going to be dancing. The first one is going to choose this large eagle bone whistle. This person is going to do good, prayers are going to be answered. The second one, very close to that but having a little bit tougher time. But this third one, this one is the lower eagle. This person is really going to have a tough year, he's already had a tough year, going to have a tough time dancing, many thoughts in a mind, many problems. This person is going to be a little bit in trouble. They are going to come in that order. So we're going to pray for all three of them, but we're going to give extra prayers for this third person. This person is going to have hard times coming."

So the first two come over and I gave them whistles and I waited. Some days later, the third person came over and said, "Boy, I really want to Sun Dance. I'm having a hard time. I need a whistle and I need some other things." I said, "Well I have a whistle, I'll give it to you if you dance." He said, "Oh yeah. I have to. I have to."

Well all three went to the Sun Dance and sure enough, sometime later this person did get into some serious trouble. But it was the interpretation of Sidney's that made me understand why I received these eagle bone whistles and who were the people that were coming. It was kind of good news and bad news with that then. I seen the results, but I didn't share it with the people that received these eagle bone whistles.

Sidney helped me a lot with my crafts. I would make a framework for a shield or a rattle or a drum then I would take it over to him and then he would go ahead and paint it. We worked on a lot of projects together. If something needed beadwork then Sandy would go ahead and do the beadwork on let's say a shield or a rattle. She and I ended up traveling to quite a few art shows so it was a group effort. I never really thought of myself as an artist and plus I like the artwork that Sidney put on there. After Sandy and I were broke up and then Sidney passed away I was kind of stuck. I really don't like to do beadwork and I don't always have enough confidence to do artwork. Eventually I ended up doing artwork but not as good as Sidney. I ended up doing some simple forms of beadwork, nothing too complicated on that but I had to do everything by myself and I pretty much still do today. My artwork has gotten a lot better.

Fifteen - Sidney Keith
Heyoka

The *heyoka* is just a person and before he got this *heyoka* business, he was just an ordinary man. You go up on the hill and get the vision to be a *heyoka*, which most of us don't like to see that vision, because it's kind of scary, because it attaches to the Thunder Beings and they're the boss over this. Whoever seeks a vision to the west and gets the vision and the Spirits say that you're gonna be a *heyoka*, well naturally that's gonna scare you, because there's a lot of things that the heyoka does that is not like the ordinary Medicine Man.

I knew three of them and one was my distant uncle at Pine Ridge. A great big fellow, but he does funny things. The horses are scared of him. He can tell a horse to do something and he'll do it. You know the medicine is that strong! Horses were scared of my uncle. Every time they have an Indian dance he's dressed a little different that the rest of them. If they dress with feathers, they probably have their bustle on this side, instead of the back. Instead of how Indians tie their hair back here, he goes around on this side and ties his. He looks funny! He dressed like the *heyoka* in the *wasicun* way. He had his clothes on backwards, because the *heyoka* is a clown. That's back when people needed clowns and this uncle was a clown. The present day Indians, they've lost everything, so they probably don't understand that, but I do know how that came about and that's through a vision.

He has to do everything backwards. Like when we go to a dance, he has to go inside the building backwards. You noticed when we went into the sweat lodge or the ceremony, we go around to the left and we go completely around and then sit down. That's the correct way of doing things, where the *heyoka* would go in and go the other way and sit down. Everybody looks at him funny, because he does that, but he can't break that rule that the Thunder Beings tell him to do it that way.

One time I was standing in a ceremony and this guy came up and it was really a nice day, no clouds. He said, "*Magajukte*. (It's gonna rain)." Then he laughed. I didn't pay attention to him. It seemed strange that he would say that but later I found out that he was a *heyoka*. So the next day it was just as nice a day again.

He knew that tomorrow was going to be a good day, because he's associated with the Thunder Beings. That's one thing that they know, these *heyokas*, they can tell you what the weather is going to be tomorrow. If the bats don't come in, they're the ones to give you a hint. They don't go out and say, "Hey, there's snow coming up." That would be telling right away. They give kind of a signal or something. You have to be *heyoka* to learn that, what they're doing.

Heyokas just look silly or funny. But nobody says anything to him, because they're scared of him. He could tell you something and it's gonna mean the opposite. That's the reason that they honor him. He comes and talks to you just like anyone else but he might say something, you might say, a premonition of what's gonna happen, even in your life. It might be a death angel coming and he'll get around to it, saying something opposite then. He knows if you're sick, you're afflicted of something and he'll direct his questions to you then, but just the opposite. Like a fellow might have TB (tuberculosis) and while they're talking he might say, if you're smoking he'll tell you not to smoke, but he'd say that smoking is good for you. Well, we'd take it the other way, that smoke is not good for you. There's something in there that's gonna raise hell. So they're smart in that way. They're not educated. The Thunder Beings tell them most of this. They sit around as if somebody's talking to them, constantly. Imagine that. They come then.

The dog is important, because *heyokas* use the dog for a ceremony, but not too often. That is the reason why we have the dog, as part of the ceremony, for the meat. The *heyoka* has got the power to stick his hand in boiling water, in the Kettle Ceremony. The *heyoka* is the only one that can handle that dog meat. He sticks his hand in there and pulls out the bone of a dog and he usually gives it to somebody, a relative or he has to take it and eat it. It's necessary. An ordinary dog that you see running around, they wouldn't eat it. I wouldn't eat one of them and I eat a lot of dogs. They're not the dogs that you see on the streets either. You've gotta be a special dog. It's gotta be a young puppy. Because the old dogs, they roam around too much. They don't like that. Things gotta be just so. They pick out a real nice puppy and they feed it real nice food and then they kill him, they choke him. They put a red *(wase)* stripe down his back to tickle to the tail and then they put a rope through around his neck and step on it and kill him that way. They never kill him with a gun, axe, or whatever, because of the Spirits overhead. You have to pray to them before you kill the dog. You don't hit him, you choke him. Because the other way's kind of brutal, you know. The Thunder Beings won't like that and they'll come shooting too with their lightning!

You never see thunder coming from the left side, they call it *catkaata* (on the left), like you go inside to your left. The thunder always comes back from the west, all the time. But if they come from the left side, from the south, southeast, you'd better watch out, because they'll blow you down! They're mad about something! That happened, because when Fools Crow was conducting the second International Sun Dance on the last day while they were dancing and blowing whistles, I looked under the Squaw Cooler and he's pointing that way, south. There was no clouds or nothing, just clear. So I asked this guy that was with him (I think it was Pete Catches) what he saw and he said, "*Miyoglasin. Iho.*" Well, that means, "mirror". So I looked over there and I could see that something was flashing. So Fools Crow came and told

Pete to get somebody, go down to the creek, where they are dancing and get some help. So he did, he got 'em.

In the meantime, I didn't know how Stanley Looking Horse knew about it. He was sitting over there and he knew what that meant. So he come and told me to tell somebody to pray. So I told him that there was already these two who were going. So they stood there, both hands towards where they saw that thing and they're praying that they don't want nothing to happen to this crowd or the people around the area. They said, "*Tunkashila* (Grandfathers)." They would call them *Tunkashila,* the Thunder Beings and the Spirits. They told them to go around us, because the storm was heading directly over Eagle Butte that was the course. Because they come in on the left side, they call it *catkaata*, you know, left side. So about the time we got through, we're trying to take our stuff down and the wind was coming from this side. Well, that means that they're blowing the storm a little farther back. Sure enough, they did! Black clouds showed up and man, they was coming fast and the wind was blowing real hard! I just had a hard time taking that teepee down in there, a great big one!

In Aberdeen that storm tipped over boxcars and raised heck down there in Fort Yates someplace. The storm turned around, then they came back to their course and kept on going, then it probably disappeared after it got so far. Fools Crow said after it was over, "They made a path for me. I'd better take off." He left right through that storm, because where he was going was straight towards that storm. I don't know how he made out, but he must have made out okay.

You know what happened that last Sun Dance we had last year? We went to the sweat lodge and we prayed that we want to have four days of good weather, real hot and humid, because these dancers have to suffer; because they don't eat, they don't drink water. It's up to the individual what they want to do. Course some of them eat, you know, but they don't eat the meat and stuff. Probably drink soup and juice, that's about all. Some of them don't even eat, they kind of stagger around after three full days!

Well anyway, on the fourth day, it didn't look too good. I got up and it was just like this, overcast, threatening to rain and I was pretty sure it was gonna rain. But I remembered that we prayed that we were gonna have a good day. So I got ready and I went down there. I had a speaker in my car, so I hooked it up and told 'em we was ready, because they were gonna pierce, starting right off the bat. I looked up and it wasn't too bad, kinda breaking up already. So everybody started getting ready and about the time we got ready and dancing, why, it kinda opened up. Yea. A few clouds go by and pretty soon it's just nice and hot again, by the time they pierced it was hot. Well, about noon my wife came down there and said, "It's still cloudy back at home." So there was something to it then.

One day this interviewer wanted to do a ceremony and I went and asked Martin High Bear if this guy could come in. Martin was in the *inipi*, but he was getting ready to leave. He said, "He wouldn't believe in this." The Spirits told him this, not to do some of these things, so that medicine has the power to tell him things, especially when he has to bring in the Pipe. But since I was going to do it anyway, I thought I would see. Martin knew that something was coming up, anybody associates with the *heyokas*, you know and he seen it differently. "I think I know who it is," he said. He didn't say who, but you know, "somebody else" means other than an Indian. But he said, "That's okay", because our church is supposed to represent all the four races of people, of color. That's the reason the Indian is never against any other race, in our old traditional way. These missionaries come in because they're nice people. People really take them in. But you see a soldier come in; they don't take them, because they come in for a different purpose, other than trying to be friends.

I'm scared of it. I don't wanna be a *heyoka*. It's good in one way, that you can see a black cloud and everybody on the shortwave radio says there's a big tornado coming. Well, when this *heyoka* hears about it, he'll get out there with a pipe and he'll pray to them. Tell them to go around and they obey him. I seen that happen a couple of times. There's one guy, he used to live down here on the river, he had a vision to be a *heyoka*, but he was more of a Christian. I think he was an Episcopal. He was a layman. Every Sunday he would go out and preach real good. He was smart and he was a good Christian, he knew a lot, but he didn't know nothing about his Indian religion. My dad was the one who knew something about it and he told him, "You better do as they say, or they'll get you." He went, "A-a-ah!" Sure enough! This big black cloud was coming and he was the only guy that had a cellar, a pretty big-sized storm cellar for that purpose. We lived about a mile and a half away. We seen it coming so we started walking towards the place. By the time we got there the wind is bad enough we should go into the cellar. Everybody comes around, all the ones that live around here, they all come around to the cellar, so we all went in the cellar. My dad told me that after we all went in the *heyoka* stood outside and kept telling my dad, "Come with me, Iyo! Iyo!" So Dad went out and looked over at this big black cloud that was rolling in. Dad asked, "What's the matter?" The *heyoka* said, "See them horsebacks coming? Black horses!" So Dad thought, "Uh-oh, I'd better get back in there." But Dad kept coaxing him. He said, "*IYO, IYO, IYO, TIMAHEL!* (Hurry inside the house!) Close that door!" But the *heyoka* he just had to stand there. He wasn't even scared of them because he was the *heyoka*, he had a vision. The wind started up and it started lightning and they got him right there! Really burned him bad! He fell down into the hole and he just went still like that, till it got farther away. This was the truth. My dad explained it to me. I was just, oh ten or twelve years old then, but I always remembered that.

They don't cure anything, but they got the power to listen to them and tell you the weather, what's gonna happen and they do funny things and say funny things they also tell you the opposite of what it's going to be. He can even tell you if you are gonna get sick tomorrow. So when he comes in, well everybody, they all kind of stare and think, "Oh, no. He's gonna tell me something bad." Ordinarily he doesn't go around doing that. But if he knows something, while you're sitting here he's going to tell you just the opposite. He's liable to tell you right in your face. So I think that's very possible and nobody wants to deal with it.

But I know another thing. I know that we can, if we see a vision like that, we can say, "*Tunkashila*, I don't want that!" Take your pipe, go on the hill, you hold your pipe to the west and you talk to them and you tell them you want something else. The Indian found that out, that he can do that. He has a choice, six options. The Indians found out that he can take any one of these four directions or Spotted Eagle or even our *nagi* under the ground. He's the one that listens to everything, because you don't stand him up on the ground. You can go over the hill someplace, where nobody can see you and he's still listening. You just can't get away. So the Indian has six options. He can take the vision from any one of the six, the four directions and heaven and earth. People might stay away from this big hill, because I think that's the reason that we don't have more of them *heyokas*, because people are scared of the vision. Ordinarily you stand like this, ready for if you see a vision you like, you say to him, "*Tunkashila*," take it, you know, smoke it and he'll make you see a vision, that's the idea. If you see a bad kind of vision, if you got a *Tunkashila* you don't like, you turn to face north, then. You see elk coming or a sacred stone, you talk to them. 'Cause you know that those are okay, the rest of them. But this other way, you better watch out! You got the heyoka power.

If a Medicine Man is a Medicine Man when he dies, why, he'll be a Spirit, but on the earth alone. You might be able to talk to him. Another Medicine Man could talk to him and say, "I'd like to have some of your power." He could stand on something someplace, out in someplace flat, with the pipe and try to commune with that man that died, that really had the good power. You can ask him too, "I'd like to have some of your power." in the *Lowanpi*, one way or another. They might have buried him, buried him with all of his equipment, like those rattles. Somehow or another, you'll find one of them in your bag!

Sixteen - Sidney Keith
Black Magic

This year there's a lot of Medicine Men up north in the Montana, Wyoming and Canada that use witchcraft and when doing the Sun Dance, they hit us three times. But Fools Crow is pretty sharp! He knows what's gonna happen. In fact, in the Indian way, they say they shot him. What they did, they sent a piece of grass, grass that's kind of hollow and I don't know how they do it, but they sent that from way up north someplace. When it came to Fools Crow, he seen it coming, so he grabbed it. He went around showing it to everybody, all the dancers. He showed it to me, so I seen it. Just a piece of brown colored grass, but it had a hole right through it, called *canka hohwa*. He gave it to Pete Catches, his helper. They prayed to the East and they prayed all the way around. He prayed to the Great Spirit. He said, "I don't want to do this. We don't want to send this back." They can do it, too. Fools Crow can send this back and **kill** that guy, whoever sent this thing. That was his purpose, to kill, but Fools Crow is powerful enough that he caught it. When he caught it, why he was looking at everybody that was sitting on that side, he would just go right up there and look at everybody. He knows who that was that sent it. In other words, he was showing his power; that he did something powerful and then he showed it to them. He gave it to Pete Catches and he wrapped it in a red cloth and at the center pole he dug a hole and stored it in there. I don't know how they do it, but they do something. That happened here at Green Grass.

    Another time at one of the dances there was an AIM member, he was dancing. Pretty soon he was holding on to his stomach and he come over to me and he said, "I've been hit." "*Hau*," I said, "Go see Fools Crow." I said to Fools Crow, "Somebody hit him with something inside." "*Hau*," he said, "come here." Well, they turned it over to Ted. So Ted went over there and took it out and the same thing, grass inside his belly. We went up and showed it towards the sun. It was about that long. Then he went up to Fools Crow and showed him. He said "We won't send it back," just like he did that first time. So Ted took him up against the pole, he took it out and buried it under the pole. Fools Crow is a believer in the Great Spirit and he's scared of things that they told him to beware of while he's on earth. That's the reason why he doesn't want to be involved in this witchcraft which these other tribes practice.

I think they got this from this occult, what they call occult, from white people abroad. I think some of these people came across, they was always going abroad, people coming in to town to talk to you. They probably discussed this with some of the best in occult. But that does something to the Spirits, too, in a different way. They probably compared notes, and the Indian thought, "I can use some of that deal to hurt somebody else." But like I say, the white man came and brought his occult and things, which all came from abroad. So the Indian is pretty smart. He goes and says, "What you got? I'll show you what I got." When he learns a few tricks, why he goes home and he uses Indian Spirits to do it for him. This is what they're doing.

We call that *hmunga*. *Hmunga*. *Kicihmunga* means to do it to somebody else. They used to do that. This happened many years ago. The best medicine men got together in a camp. They sit around and do their thing. Somebody can *hmunga* somebody across the camp and he'll in turn, do something to him. They're having a contest to see who's the best one, the strongest! So not many years ago, maybe after the white man came, this occult business came in. The first time, I don't know when it was. My grandfathers, they used to talk about these things, about how good a man was that knew how to do them. Say you're riding a fast horse and the Medicine Man does something to that horse so that it falls with you. It won't hurt you, but makes that horse fall. When it gets to you it just falls. They knew that this guy was doing it. So if you're a Medicine Man you can think up a better one than that, and send it back! That's sort of a contest that's going around and around. You see, in those days they didn't use it to kill each other, they were just competing against each other.

I went up to that dance at Eagle Butte a few weeks back. I took my little grandson; he dances, so we dressed him up. We couldn't find a place to sit down, and I forgot to bring a chair. So I said, "You go and just dance around here, don't go in the middle." So I was sitting there by the drummers, just sitting like this and the drum was right there and he was dancing around. I knew this guy that was facing me, I knew him, he's not a singer, he's a dancer. He's sitting there and he looked at me, said, "*He makutelo*" (I'm shot). I knew what that meant, somebody hit him with something. That's what they mean when they say, "*Hmunga.*" So I said, "*Hwo*" (How is it?). He said, "*Lila mahpiya*" (Very cloudy, not good). So right away, I thought of *sinkpe tawote*. Just about that time the music stopped and the guy come over to talk to us. "Hey," he says, "I'm having a real tough time." So this guy asked one of the drummers if they had any *sinkpe*. "I'd have to go back to the car," he says.

In the meantime my little grandson had to go to the bathroom so I said, "We'll have to go clear to the house." About a quarter of a mile, then he didn't want to go back to the dance again (chuckling). We got in the car, went back to the house: he went to the bathroom, and I took a bunch of *sinkpe* in my pocket. My grandson wanted to stay, so I told him he could stay. But I went back up there.

I gave the drummer about that long a strip (gesturing, indicating about 2-3 inches of the root) and the dancer, I know him too, so I gave him some. I had a bunch in my pocket. I sensed that they were doing something, something like that, so I kind of hung around there, but nothing else happened. But they do that. Like say, if I was a Medicine Man, and you was a good dancer, but there was one guy that was a better dancer than you are, "Get me a pipe," I'd say, "I'm gonna throw... uh... not do anything bad...just see that they misstep or something." So, that's what happens, he uses one of his Spirits to do that. They shouldn't do that, but it happens. It's illegal. I keep telling them all, I say, "You can't do that." When they do that it makes a dancer *gicicetu* (stumble or misstep). They shoot each other with that, just to win. Oh, it's just a little weed. It's about that small (indicating the last joint on the little finger). It's *canhlogan*, that's what they call it. Ya, it's usually about that long. It's called, just a needle, *tahinspa*. That's what they use. They shoot it, they shoot you with it. When they hit you, it's imaginary. When it hits you, the thing falls off: but that thing stays in, you can't see it. So, if you dance, why, your mind is not up to it, so you get out of step. That's the way it works, and that's what they call *hmunga*, black magic, witchcraft.

So anyways, I think they're using it up north, Canada, Montana. But the Sioux haven't used it. 'Cause we're against this peyote, too! We're against it. That's no good, either. That originated in Mexico. They use this peyote stuff that comes from the cactus plant. It makes you, if you drink it, why you get hallucinations. And that church, whatever church it is, they use that peyote, now they are using a pipe with it. Saying their things to the Great Spirit, which is baloney! The witchcraft is also baloney to our Sioux, but they're doing it, you know.

Seventeen - Melvin Miner
Indian Land for Sale

We are lucky here in Rapid because we have an Indian Hospital. A full functioning hospital, it's not just a health center, it's actually a hospital. It's one of the reasons we have a lot of Indian people here. Some go to an area that has jobs. Here we have some jobs, but we do have a hospital to take care of your illnesses. So that's a big plus in this community, plus it's the largest employer of Indian people. It so happened I was Chairman of the Rapid City Indian Health Advisory Board, five out of the ten years I was on the board. We're a board that advises the hospital plus we run our own programs.

Our G.S.A. area office is in Aberdeen, South Dakota. They informed our board and the hospital that there was five acres of land within this forty acres the hospital sits on, that was going to be put up for sale. Of course that kind of disturbed some of us because we said, "Look at the hundreds and hundreds and hundreds of acres, maybe even thousands, which have been taken and utilized for city or state or federal reasons. They basically found a way to take that land from us and now our own people are trying to sell five more acres?"

I started noticing that there wasn't a sweat lodge available around Rapid City. There might have been one somewhere, but I didn't know about it. I went to my father in law and told him about the sale and the idea of a sweat lodge on the property. I *opagied* or offered him tobacco and said, "We had a lot of Indian land here in Rapid City and a lot of reasons why we lost that land. There are churches on that land. Sioux Park is on that land. National Guard Armory is on that land. Schools are on that land. All that acreage and the only thing that is left is forty acres which Sioux San Hospital sits on."

He sat there for a while and here he said "Here's what we'll do. This land is going to be sold, in a month or two months. What the Spirits have told me is to put a sweat lodge on that five acres. The sweat lodge is a healing type of ceremony and Sioux San Hospital should cooperate with that. Even though there's gonna be some problems we're going to run into, just the idea of a sweat lodge in Rapid City and at a very visible location and then to top it off is that some of the administrators are probably not people that go to sweat lodges."

I don't believe I told the board. What I did was write up a contract and presented it to the unit director. I said that this plan could be either be with the Rapid City Indian Health Advisory Board or with myself to put a sweat lodge on this land. I said for religious purposes and for healing. It was rejected by the service unit director. He said, "Well I have several problems with the wording. This one says religion. We can't have that, so you have to scratch that out of there and keep the healing part." He said that would be key and then we actually made the contract with the Rapid City Indian Health Advisory Board, because somebody actually had to be responsible for this. So our first mission was to get that okayed fairly quickly, I'm gonna say within like three weeks.

I went over to our treatment program (it's basically the twelve step treatment) and I met with the director and some of the staff and told them that we're going to build a sweat lodge over here. I need some volunteers from your clients if that could happen. Also, when this is completed we want to implement the sweat lodge into your healing program. They weren't fully sold on that idea but they provided the workers. I think there were six or seven guys, they came over. We also had some community people that came and participated in the making of that sweat lodge. We had picks, shovels all kinds of tools. We dug a pit. We had some of the guys digging and it was summertime. It was almost all stone up there, sparks flying all over because it wasn't just dirt. We had to have a windbreak so we had to build a corral. We ended up going to this one organization, Indian Relief Council. They provided the money to buy the wood, the poles, the nails and some tarps. We had a windbreak; we had the pit so we went and got the willows. All of this was probably done in about five days.

The next step was we had Sidney come up and bless the sweat lodge. He did a ceremony and I remember the interpretations. Part of the interpretation is the sweat lodge is going to serve our community in prayer and in healing; hundreds and thousands of people are going to come and use this. This is something that every community needs to be a positive community. We have a hospital here, but this is going to be on that level, healing in a spiritual way and praying, they are going to work together. Also this is going to work together with the treatment center. A lot of our people were going to treatment to overcome their alcohol and drug problems; this would be implemented to work with that.

The land went up for sale and not one person bid on the land. When I called Aberdeen, one dollar would have bought five acres of land up there. There were no bids at all put on the land. If there was, if they had tried to sell it we were going to take it to court under the Freedom of Religious Act. I think we would have had a good case. But we didn't need to go through that.

When I started that project I thought that to do this, it would take a long time but it took off very quickly. We got the property and the sweat lodge built so people could use it, we just asked them to clean up, you know, its public, the next person who is going to use it won't find anything broken or trashed or anything. Everybody pretty much knew that already, so you could go up there and use it as long as somebody else wasn't using it. Finally we came up with a form that we wanted people to sign up on. We were not really trying to control what is going on over there, just saying if we had some opposition from I.H.S. or the community or something that we could at least show how many times this has been used and estimate how many individuals have used this. Sidney played the key role in the Black Hills Pow Wow and in the sweat lodge for Rapid City.

Eighteen - Melvin Miner
Curing a Spiritual Leader

One day we got a call from someone who said that they would like to have Sidney go see a certain person. It looked like this person was having a hard time when we went to the house. It looked like this person was shaking. Sidney smudged this person with sage and maybe sweetgrass and was sitting there. Then he said, "This is a spiritual illness." What happened was that this person accepted a pipe as an offering for somebody who wanted to go up on the hill. They were from another state and this spiritual person did not make it over there to put this person up. For whatever reason this spiritual person started to feel some things going wrong around him. There were several things that weren't going in his favor like something was trying to tell him something. He was starting to shake and he couldn't function very well. The interpretation was that the spiritual person who received this pipe, who was shaking, did not fulfill their part of a vow to put this other person up on the hill. This person who wanted to go up on the hill made a vow and couldn't complete that vow because the spiritual person wasn't there. So it fell on this Medicine Man too, as a reminder to keep that vow of if you accept the pipe or if you give your word that you have to follow through with that. If not, then they were going to remind you that you had a job to do and that is one of the reasons why you are given this ability and responsibility. So they talked it over, they talked about it and the spiritual person said, "I remember now and I'll take care of this." Shortly after that this person was back on his feet and well. Within a month or so this person came over, he wanted to do a *wopila*. So we had a *wopila* ceremony at our house. We set the altar up and the person came in and prayed, gave thanks for the help and then went and took care of the business that they were supposed to take care of.

    I do recall one incident when Sidney asked me to go over to a person's house, he couldn't do it himself. Someone called him and said they had an injury or infection or something. He said, "I want you to go over there. Accept that tobacco. Then tell them what to do." I was like *no problem* on the outside. In my mind I was like **what**? I mean I was not sure if I was capable of this.

Well I went to the person's house. He came out and I said, "Sidney couldn't make it." He handed me a cigarette. The instant that cigarette went into my hand, I could see a picture in my head. The image of an infection, because that was what I seen, clear as day, just like watching TV. I told the person, "Put some tobacco and some sage on the infection and wrap it up." I told that person quick, just as soon as the tobacco hit my hand, "Put tobacco on there. Put sage on there. This will draw the infection out. Then keep on repeating that until it's healed." You know, nothing major. But the power that he gave me at that time was to see how he sees certain things, maybe not everything, because Spirits talk to him. But this was just as clear as if I was watching TV. He only allowed me to do that once, that one time, but I got a small glimpse into how they operate: what happens, what they see and it's very clear with that.

Most of the time with Sidney we had a lot of sweat lodges. Sidney was very healthy maybe a little bit overweight, but we could still do the sweats. When he started to get grey hair we noticed that we were having more and more house ceremonies, the ceremony would be performed in the house. It was just that the sweat lodge was a little bit tough for him to get in and get out of and harder to sit in there comfortably during the sweat, because of the heat of the sweat lodge. But I know you could learn quite a bit at these sweat lodges. I remember one time somebody had several old injuries that were on their leg. The person wasn't there in the ceremony for these injuries, but they said that they had a broken leg from before and they still felt a lot of pain. Sidney would take ashes and he would draw with his finger in the ashes a dragonfly on that injured part of that body and this was a technique that he said was very simple but very effective. It would start to heal right away. The dragonfly is a healer type of insect, but also it works with the west direction. The dragonfly has a lot of healing powers to it even though it's real small. We saw this done several times and it worked. We used to do this to my son when he would be a pitcher and his arm would be hurting. We would take some ashes and then draw the symbol of this dragonfly on his arm so he could go longer with the pitching.

There were quite a few ceremonies held out in Lakota Homes. There's about 200 homes with about an average of five people per house, they have 2, 3, 4 bedroom homes. So there are about a thousand people out there and the majority are Lakota's. There was a ceremony planned and my cousin and me, we didn't know about this ceremony throughout the daytime. About 5 o'clock, one of the family members came over and said, "Hey. Joe Chiona is gonna do a ceremony if you guys would like to attend." My cousin was a singer, I could sing a little bit, but he knew the songs so we went to it. It was probably like an hour later. They had the room all closed off and all dark in there. Joe was sitting in the middle with his altar set up. So we turned off the lights to start the ceremony.

One of the people that was sitting by the door where the lights were, all of a sudden we heard him yell and he was saying, "Let me down! Sorry! Have pity on me!" We could hear it was like it was coming from the ceiling. He stopped and we knew it was over there by the door so the Medicine Man said, "What's going on?" The person said, "Somebody lifted me up and my head touched the ceiling three or four times. Not real hard but I know that something's wrong." So Joe said, "What might be wrong?" He said, "I might have smoked marijuana today." Joe said, "Well you know you can't do that and come to a ceremony. The Spirits are probably mad at you." So that person left.

So Joe started over. Pretty soon this girl was crying and a drumstick that the singer was using was taken away and that drumstick was not beating on her but was hitting her in a way that she was feeling pretty bad. That's usually a sign that something's not good. So we stopped the ceremony again. Joe said, "What's wrong?" The girl said, "That drumstick is hitting me." Joe said, "Why is that? Is something wrong?" She said, "Well I'm on my time." Joe said, "Well, you know you shouldn't be in here if you are on your time." She said, "Well I brought sage!" Joe said, "Well that's not going to protect you!" So she said that she was sorry for that mistake and didn't mean any harm. So *she* left.

So then we were going on with the ceremony and there was some rattles and these rattles came right up to my cousin and me right before we were going to pray. Something didn't seen right. Joe asked us, "Did *you* make a mistake today? What did *you* do today?" My cousin and me, we wasn't using drugs, wasn't doing alcohol. We couldn't think at the moment. I was like, "I don't know." Joe said, "Well, where did you go today?" I remembered my cousin and me; we would go to this bar to play pool during lunchtime and then grab a sandwich and then I'd go back to work. Here we did that that day, not knowing we were going to have a ceremony that night. But he told us that wasn't right. That even being in a bar or a liquor store on the day of a ceremony, you shouldn't go to the ceremony. We told him we didn't know that but that we learned something that we wouldn't do again.

So we went on with the ceremony and pretty soon we noticed that the man in the middle, Joe C. was in some commotion there. He was getting bothered and here he admitted to us in the circle, "I made a mistake today too. They're showing their frustration towards me. I have rules. Of course I have rules; we all do to these ceremonies. How we conduct ourselves before, during and after." So the Spirits, they didn't let nobody off the hook that night. We all learned something, we all caught hell.

We had ceremonies at the house a lot. At least one a week we would have one. There would be people coming in from all over. Many of them were Sun Dancers from the Sun Dance Sidney ran up in Green Grass. So there were a lot of people that we knew. They would come and some of them would want ceremonies. I remember one that we had there. While we are in the ceremony it's protected with tobacco ties, the sweetgrass, the cedar and the sage. But there was a Spirit that came one night that was waiting outside. Sidney said, "There is a Spirit outside and he's a Spaniard. The Spaniard was buried alive down in South America. He said they were fighting and that something caved in and as it caved in he was still alive and he died later after so many days. But he asked for forgiveness for what he was doing. An earthquake or something opened up the place where he had been for five hundred years and he started walking up from South America. He went to a couple of tribes in the Southwest and he stayed around. He was trying to help out and he moved on. He ended up at our front door. He said that he wanted to help out; that he knew about Lakota's through speaking with other Spirits. He said that if someone is willing to take him, offer him to come to their house that he would go and he would watch over their children and the property. So one family said, "Sure. We'll go ahead and try it." So they left.

Later I talked to both the man and wife and I said, "How are things going?" "Oh they're going good. He comes around; he moves things, walks through the house, things like this. But sometimes we wake up and he pulls the covers off of us. He wakes us up." So they weren't happy about some of the things that was going on, thinking he was getting bored or something. So at another ceremony, they asked if he would leave and go on to another family or help somebody else out. He was outside and said that he would go so he went ahead and left at that time. I haven't run into that since, where a Spirit other than that of an Indian person coming into a ceremony.

Nineteen - Sidney Keith
Martin High Bears Vision

All the medicine men had visions, but not all of them are the same and Martin has one that's kind of unique. Felix explained it real well. I used to go to his ceremonies and he tells his a little different. Martin also tells it a little differently because they don't all see the same thing.

Martin went and faced west. He said that there was a man that came. He had a blanket and feather and he was coming and the clouds were like a turmoil that he was walking in, just waist high, a kind of a cloud underneath. He couldn't see his face and every time he opened his eyes, sparks flew, like lightning. He stopped a little ways away and he talked to him and he, because they're the boss, he said, *"What do you want, friend?"* or *kola*. Remember, we used that many times in this thing? *Kola*. It means friend. It means a closer friend than the *wasicun* (white man) interpretation, so *kola* means quit a bit to the Indian. That's why he asked, *"Kola, what do you want?"* So that starts the thing, because him being the boss, he wants to find out what Martin wants. So then he tells him what he wanted. He wants to humble himself in the presence of the Spirits, the main Spirits, the commanding Spirits. And he wants his people to live and live right on the earth, between the heaven and earth. They always refer to it that way, because after all we live between the heaven and earth. The way we live is, the Great Spirit is watching us and the Mother is listening underneath. The Spotted Eagle looks down and watches over us, too. So he tells him that and he said, "*Waste lo. That's good, that you ask me.*"

Then he turns to the north and offers his pipe to it. On that side the Indian with the red blanket comes out of the north and also the sacred stones are coming. That's the ones he sees that spark. A bunch of them come from that direction, because they watch that direction. They also asked, "*Taku icahan? Niye cin*? (*What do you want friend?*)" So he tells him that he wants to be a Medicine Man and to heal the people and he wants something.

When you say that, you get a stone, like I did. You get a stone and that's the one that talks to you when you do the ceremony. I think he has three or four, Martin has. He never shows any. I think he has them in a pocket like this. Remember I had that little bag? I gave that to him. That was my stone. He set it in there. That's the one that talks to me, or I didn't do it right at that time, but he did talk to me. I just left him there so he could talk to Martin, you see.

The Eagle always comes to me first, that I don't understand, but that's the way it always happens. I always expect that. The deer always comes, the black-tailed deer that's in there. Sometimes he just sits on my lap and I hate to touch him, because I feel that I'm not that good, or not humble or I'm too straight forward. But I can feel his hair on my hand. It's really soft, like a deer and when he goes off, he makes a noise like that, hoofs on the floor. You heard that in there. They come and they can hear them talk, "Ba-a-a," just like a little sheep! That's a black-tail deer. He does that all the time, too. You know that Martin has control of his black tail-deer. He tells him things, you know.

But anyway that's what you ask for, whatever you want to do, to be a Medicine Man to doctor sick people. All this is "*Waste Lo!*" It's all good.

Then this way, east, he said there was a man coming on that side over here. Somehow he fell down and they was looking at him, he didn't even move. Could have sworn he was dead. Then here come a bunch of buffalos in the distance. A cloud of dust and buffalos and they stuck their head on the ground and they flipped it up as they come. When they got close, why he knew that those were the herbs, these buffalos were digging it up. They had a man come along picking the herbs up and he had a bowl of water, he put them in there, he was mixing it up as he came along. When he got to this man that was laying there, he had to hold his head up like that and give him a drink. He was dead, like that and he went by and he couldn't see him, then he just disappeared. But he stood there and watched and here this man got up and walked away. So the buffalo had lots to do with the medicine, all different kinds of medicine to heal people. So Martin said, "I want some of that to use to heal my people." He said, "*Waste Lo!*" That's good, you know.

    Then he said he faces south and that a Spirit, a *wanagi*, comes walking and lots of birds come, all shapes and sizes! This man has two rattles, so he knew that he was gonna be a Medicine Man. But he also had a skull, a buffalo skull. At these ceremonies we use a buffalo skull, to put on the west bank facing east, 'cause the buffaloes they came from that way and she brought the Pipe from the west, the Calf Pipe woman did. The Spirit from the south tells them, *"This is the way you're gonna do it. This is the way you're gonna make a design. This is the way you put up your flags and this is the way you're gonna sing."* So he said, *"Waste lo!"* That's good! So that now he's good enough to stand there three or four days.

This is the way it has been told to me. The visions that have the rattles, they reaffirm his belief that he's gonna be a Medicine Man. Then he holds the Pipe up and he hears somebody up there! The voice said, *"You're a good man. You've got the power to stand up and call us. We'll listen. We'll come to you. All the directions will come to you. Waste lo."* Then he points his pipe towards the earth and somebody hits him on the sole of his foot and the voice says, *"I hear everything. When you go over the hill to hide, I can hear you. Dig a hole a hundred feet down and hide, I can still hear you. You fly up there thousands of miles and I can still hear you. You can't get away from me that way. When you say 'Waste lo', when you holler I'll be the first one to hear and I'll tell the rest of the Spirits and the Wanbli Gleska will see you."*

That's the way he told it, the whole vision, as he stands in all the directions. That's the vision that they tell when the Spirits will come. After he raises his Pipe first to each direction, he prays to them. First he said, "Remember you told me if I do this you are gonna come and see me. I'm praying tonight that you do that." He points it over there and says the same thing and then he tells his vision, so that's the way that they made him see it. Then he repeats it to remind them that they told him that if he does it that way, that they'll come and see him. After they turn the lights off, well they come and see him. I'm no Medicine Man, but I seen him do it that way and that's the way it's supposed to be. That all took place last year, but Martin was with Felix all the time. He was his helper, his right hand man, you call it. I think that Felix was coaching him all the time. That's just the way they do it. That builds up your confidence and like me, my teacher's Fools Crow.

Well you see, he saw that vision and they told him that if he faced to the four directions, they'd come-a-running and being as a red man, there has to be four red flags instead of some other color. But you have the right colors on others than the four. That's the only reason they have four red ones, but that represents the Spirits, the *wanagi* (soul) that's associated with the Indians. The Spirits can only talk Indian. I think now they understand English! That's pretty good. But the reason you go up on the hill and prayed, go through all this and stood up there four nights, four days without food or water and prayed and prayed and they'd make you see a vision. They talk to you. But you don't understand it, so you don't know what happens. After you come back down, you tell your sponsor what you saw and they know what you are talking about. That happens a lot of times. Just last year these (name omitted) boys they like the culture so much, they thought they'd do it. The Spirits talked to them, but they don't understand Sioux very well. So naturally, they saw things and heard things, but that was it. They weren't the ones that the Spirits will talk to. You have to be a real Indian, like me, full blood. In fact, they follow me around the house, trying to talk to me, but I'm still, I'm just an amateur at it, you might say!

He's also drawing that vision and the *Iktomi*, that's where he comes in and he watches over this altar, the *Iktomi* does. He comes in first and looks at that design to see if it's done right and that's all he does.

Remember he was standing there, he was praying to a direction. Then he says, "*Hau, hau.*" Somebody started in talking to him. That's *Iktomi*, he's saying that. He's telling them, "*Okay, Waste lo, you did alright.*" But sometimes he forgets something, one little mark on there. "*Hau, Hau,*" he keeps saying that and he'll turn around and he'd do it; he'd mark it, just like he showed him. So the *Iktomi* comes in first and tells him that he seen that little altar for him, that's part of his vision. He comes and looks it over and he tells him it's right while he's praying. So that's why he's saying, "*Hau, Hau.*" Even with the lights on they come and talk to you.

Twenty - Melvin Miner
Dogs

We lived two different places in Lakota Homes, but at one of them we had a dog behind our house. It was summertime and I remember the dog was kind of acting funny. We had him chained up. There were a lot of packs of dogs at the time that were running around and some of them had mange and some of them had distemper. They were getting into peoples garbage and kind of raising Cain with the kids.

The dog made a noise one day and Sidney was sitting at the kitchen table and I was sitting there. He said, "Your dog just told me that he wants to die. He wants to go now. He's sick." I said, "Oh really?" He said, "Yeah. But he wants to go in an Indian way or a spiritual way." So I asked him what that was. He said, "Take a plastic bag and then put that in your back pocket. "He was maybe getting distemper, because he was getting kind of defensive when you would approach him. He said, "Take that red paint and start from the top of his head and go all the way down between his eyes to his nose." I said, "I don't know if he'll stay still." He says, "No. He's requesting this." So I got the paint out. Sidney was the artist. We always had paint in our house and he always had paint at his. So I went out there and I approached the dog and the dog was standing up and I looked in his eyes and his eyes were really glassy. I thought he was going to bite me. He was kind of a big dog, no particular breed.

So I approached him. Sidney said to pray as you do this, so I talked to the dog. I said, "Sorry for the disease. We're going to grant your wish." So he stood still and I painted him. I took the plastic bag out and I told him that this was going to cut off the breath of life. He stood there and I put the plastic bag over his head and tightened it. He moved his head around but he didn't bite or nothin'. I kept it on probably 5 minutes and he died right there. Then Sidney said, "Find a place to bury him. Bury him a couple feet down. Put some tobacco there and pray for his Spirit. Thank him for being a companion to our family, protecting us." So I did. I took him north of town and I buried him and prayed with the tobacco.

Sometime later Sidney was telling me that he had a dream about a dog that came to him in his dream. He said this dog spoke to him. This dog represents the west direction. The west direction is like the *wakiyans*, the thunder, the lightning, the thunderbird, hail, rain, horse, wolf, coyote and this dog. He said this dream was telling him that this dog is a very close relative of ours. Just like the buffalo was. This dog is by far the most domestic relative we have. It protected us. It warned us of danger. We're talking 100's of years ago. Going way back before the horse and that the dog was strong enough it could drag a travois. We could load things on to or if it was strong enough, we could put like a saddle on it, with saddlebags and it could carry our items. It protects our kids. Kids learn about the four legged through this animal. He said what this dog talked to him about or showed him in this dream. He said:

"Us Lakota's, we can't be treating these dogs mean, can't be kicking them or hitting them. We can't be starving them, neglecting them, abusing them. They were sent here to us to help us and they have. They have a long history with us and even though they don't have those duties no more, they paid their dues. Remember this; I'm going to tell people that it's appropriate to treat their dog, their horse and these animals like they're a member of the family. In return they will help your family. So, you

feed your family everyday. Feed the Spirits everyday. Feed your dog everyday and good things will come from that."

Of course in the Kettle Ceremony a Medicine Man who works with that west direction, sometimes they require a puppy or a dog to be boiled. They would have to choke the dog or smother it, not shoot it or stab it or anything like that. This young puppy would be used to go along with that ceremony. Ever who sponsors this ceremony is looking for help from that Medicine Man and his Spirits so this dog plays an important role for *heyokas* in their ceremonial rituals and duties. That's kind of where some people get this idea that we eat dog. They think that we eat it all the time. This would be one instance where we would eat probably just a little piece of a dog 'cause it's good to share the little puppy with everybody that comes to the ceremony. Also there's not much meat on a little puppy anyhow. But the only other time this would happen is through harsh famine a long time ago, where maybe a blizzard came in a long winter and with not enough food and there's a possibility that you would eat your dog or horse in order to survive. Those are extreme cases but today it does go on as far as the dog ceremony some Medicine Man do perform that ritual.

The next story I'm about to tell is about a family. Jimmy DuBrey was going to have surgery in Minnesota and they had a dinner for him and a prayer ceremony. He went to have his surgery and treatment up there, then he came back to Pine Ridge Reservation. But they had relatives up here and we went there to sing and he was giving a *wopila*, a dinner. It was at a school and I think it had to have been on a Saturday or a Sunday in the evening. He thanked everybody. He wanted to give a few gifts away. He said everything was going good for him. They had a drum group his family is really known for. There were some others there, so they sung some songs and then he brought out his pipe and we smoked it.

That night I was at my house. I was in my bedroom sleeping and I heard someone say, "Melvin. Melvin." I had the covers pulled up, it was kind of cold and I was covered up pretty good. I looked up over the blankets and on my window, was this stringy kind of lightning, all over my window. I looked at it and I was blinking a lot and it was real bright. Then I saw an animal in the middle. Then I saw two war clubs or drumsticks beside that animal. The animal was looking at me and then it turned sideways and it was a dog. Then all of a sudden it went away and I went back to sleep. I woke up the next day and I told my father-in- law about it. He said, "Well, that was a good ceremony that happened the other day with Jimmy DuBrey."

Shortly after that I was working in that same room. I actually moved out the bed in that room to make it into a work room and I was working in there. I had another helper; Martin Long Soldier who was in there helping me work on something. The southwest corner of that room from the ceiling down to about my waist, a string of sparkles came. It was daytime and the only way I can describe it is like on the Fourth of July, the sparkles that come off a sparkler, how it looks like its falling. It looked like it came from out of nowhere, like out of the ceiling and came straight down just sparking! I looked right away 'cause it was about a foot away from me and Martin Long Soldier who was there too. We both looked and he said, "What's that?" "I don't know." I said. Then I remembered what else took place in that room sometime before that. That one I kept to myself. I didn't ask what the interpretation of that was. But I've never seen anything like that happen in the daytime since then.

Twenty One - Melvin Miner
Indian Names

I know Sidney has given Indian names, Lakota names, to some young people. I remember asking him how he determines that and he said usually it comes in a dream and the Spirits will show him. I remember him telling me that he had a dream of two flowers; one was a sunflower and one a rose. A lady asked him to name her two daughters so that was the names he gave to them. Also the Spirits would tell Sidney a name. The family would go ahead and *opagi* him tobacco (offer him tobacco or a loaded pipe) for this, for the name is especially important. It's really the Spirits who give this individual their name and has something to do with their personality or something they might become in the future or some trade of their life, how they are going to live, so it's very important. So you have your Christian name and then you'll have a spiritual name. I had a cousin who passed away; he didn't have a spiritual name so we went to a sweat. The Medicine Man gave him a name in the *inipi*. So there's a few ways to get this name, either it can be handed down through a relative that

A Common Man

passes away and so they would hand that name down to you so you could carry that on.

Back on Cheyenne River Sioux Reservation they have an annual Labor Day celebration, Pow Wow, art show, rodeo, all of these activities. As we were leaving the Pow Wow grounds we were shaking hands with people as we would see them; have some small talk with them. There was this individual and his wife and as we were shaking hands and my wife said, "You remember *so-and-so* and his wife." The father-in-law said as he was shaking her hand, "Sure. You're the ones with twins?" And then she kind of blushed a little bit and she said, "No." He goes, "No? Oh, sorry." And then we went back to the house. Eight months later she had twins. We asked him about it and he said the Spirits told him to say that and she probably thought at that moment that he mistook her for somebody else but actually he was kind of giving her a clue to that she would have twins coming up. So, I suppose other Medicine Man have that ability to tell a woman what they are going to have.

I have another story that I wasn't there for but Sidney was telling me, this was before 1980. He said a reporter gave him a call one day. The reporter wanted to come and see him. I'm not sure of the reporter, sounded like he was from out of state. This reporter said, "I've heard a lot about Sioux Medicine Men and your name came up and that's why I called you. I want to know if these things are for real. I hear you guys have Spirits and you guys can heal people." Sidney said, "We can't show off. We can't charge money, you know we have rules. This is a sacred gift that the Spirits, they decide if they are going to help out or not. They are much wiser than any of us. So come on over and we'll go outside of town." This was up in Eagle Butte, Cheyenne River. He said, "We went out to an isolated place. I told the reporter, 'I have an eagle song and I sang that song. The eagle that works with me showed up and he was flying up above. I told the reporter, 'I don't want you to take a picture but there it is.' The reporter looked and looked and he said, 'I can't see it.' I said, well, it's there." He didn't want to tell the reporter that if that eagle had some reason it would not to show himself to this man. Maybe he was going to do something with it. The reporter really wasn't convinced when he left, but Sidney said Spirits have rules and they have reasons and for whatever reason the reporter couldn't see the eagle. But Sidney said the eagle was there. So Sidney said after that "If somebody wanted me to show him something like this, I went ahead and refused those kinds of requests. They would have to go to a ceremony or they would have to *hanbleceya* out to do these ceremonies to see something. But the Spirits know why you are there and if they show you something that's up to them, that's not up to me on that."

Sidney was telling me and it's not a good story 'cause I don't know if these people are still living, but there was this man who called him on the phone and said he had a daughter who her legs were paralyzed and she couldn't walk. I'm not sure if she was born that way or if she had an accident. He said that he heard that he was a good Medicine Man and that he might be able to help his daughter out. Sidney said, "Come on up we'll see. Bring her up."

He said maybe about a week later, this man came up with his daughter and he was praying over the daughter. When they left and she went home, the father called back. He said that one leg worked, the other one didn't. The man was a little upset about that. He said, "Why both legs couldn't be healed?"

Sidney said the man came up with his daughter trying to help her but the man had alcohol on his breath. He was drinking that day and for that, since he didn't do all that could have been done to make that prayer 100 per cent successful, his daughter was only healed 50 per cent. Because of her prayer and his actions had averaged out to 50 per cent. He had to explain to this man that that was all he could do under those circumstances and that the Spirits have rules.

The rules for ceremonies are for the women, they just can't be in their time and they can't attend until after. Also you can't be using drugs or alcohol, especially on that day. So they are simple rules, but if you have an alcohol problem or a drug problem sometimes that's a challenge for somebody to stay sober all day. So it's a sad story because the young girl could be walking today. If you abide by those rules, quite obviously you have to have some respect for somebody that you are trying to help. In this case this guy was trying to help his daughter, but he did not abide by the rules, so an innocent victim like her came out on the short end.

Another sweatlodge I remember was here in Rapid City. This one guy named Ken and me had, I wouldn't say an argument, but somehow we had some words and it just happened to be the day of the sweat lodge. We were still working together but somebody must have said something or did something. I didn't seem that bad, but when you're in the sweat lodge you can't be getting into an argument or anything like that. I brought the stones into the sweat lodge, they were glowing red. I sat down by the door. I was about ready to close the door and I seen Sidney reach into the pit where the stones are and he picked up a stone and he held it in his left hand and he grabbed Ken who was sitting next to him. He grabbed him on the wrist and Ken started crying. Then he let go of him and he put that stone in his right hand and he grabbed my wrist and emotionally I started crying. He gave us a little speech about how every day we should not argue, but especially not have hard feelings at a sweat lodge or a ceremony. The thing that was so amazing about it was that he was holding this super hot rock in his hand and it didn't bother him. But also what it did to us, it really made us, Ken and me, it really humbled us quickly.

Twenty Two - Melvin Miner
Treaties

Throughout the years the issue of the Black Hills Treaty has come up. There have been many treaty meetings. There's a lot written about the Black Hills claim from the Great Sioux Nation especially in the Indian newspapers. People speak about it a lot. I asked Sidney to comment on it. He said, "I know this is where our people come from, I agree with our ancestors who passed on these stories that this world was created and then we came from the Star Nation as a Spirit into the Black Hills, into Wind Cave. We lived as a Spirit. We were told to stay there until we got direction from the Great Spirit. Then Iktomi spoke through the opening of Wind Cave and told us how beautiful it was out here. We should come out and enjoy this, there is light and it's not dark. As a people we could see and we could speak to each other. This is why we say that our language is sacred, for we were still in the sacred form when we learned our language. We decided that we would go out, so we left Wind Cave. That's when we realized that when we were down in Wind Cave we didn't have to eat food, didn't have to drink water, because we were semi-divine in Spirit form. So these were new responsibilities, to clothe ourselves, feed ourselves, to hunt, take care of ourselves and our children. Everyday we had to do these things, as a people to survive. It was very rough. Then we made a pact with the buffalo, the four legged relative of ours that he would take care of us. He would provide us with everything. We take what we need, we say thanks to him. We pray to the Great Spirit for teaching us how to deal with life, on taking, giving and receiving on the protocol of that.

    Well that puts us in the Black Hills. No other tribe claims their creation story out of the Black Hills but we do and we have passed that down through generations and generations. When the time came there were two parties as far as the Lakota's and the other Indian tribes that were at this Fort Laramie Treaty of 1868, that other party being the U.S. government. When we sat down to work out this treaty agreement there was a Sacred Pipe involved. This pipe was filled, not the sacred one, but a pipe and it was more of a peace pipe. This pipe was loaded with a prayer and it was understood that it was smoked to seal this treaty with the Black Hills, that we should have the Black Hills and this land around it because it's our homeland. That's spelled out in the treaties and both sides smoked the pipe. Because of that, the Spirits were involved in the Black Hills treaty and they can't be lied to. They will help us in getting this Black Hills back or letting us have access to it. They will continue to be there for us, working with us.

Sidney believed that this pipe played a major role in this treaty for the Black Hills. He said there is always hope, there is always hope for that. He says no matter if we made a bad decision somewhere in there and we were forced to agree on a lot of it from under duress or we were deceived or tricked because of the language and interpretation. But we knew the pipe and we knew that it would protect us, protect our people. So it was good that we brought the pipe to that treaty. There was probably other pipes, from other tribes, hopefully there was.

Sidney said that he thought this constant struggle would go on. Because there is a lot of talk from our people about, "Well we're gonna never get back the Black Hills. Maybe we should go ahead and accept the money." But he never thought that our people would do that; even through real hard times or even through the distance in time. He hoped that we would keep passing down the word not to sell the Black Hills, onto our children and our grandchildren that we must hang on to it. So that was the answer that he gave me.

We've had a problem with racism in South Dakota, especially through the years of the 1970's all the way up to now. Well maybe this racism was going on in the 1960's too. There are problems all over, not only with Indian people, but with people of different nationalities. But here in Rapid City and in this state it's mainly Native American. More and more people were starting to get more involved with the issues in this community. There were Health issues with the hospital, housing issues up in Lakota Homes and the government of Rapid City kind of looked at them as two different problems. There were also issues with education, it seemed like a lot of our children were dropping out or getting kicked out and a there were a lot of complaints: some on the administrators; some on the teachers; some with the other students, but it seemed like a very high rate.

There were some incidents that caused the community here to gather and to start organizing to show our children that we care about them, that we would voice our concern as a group. We decided we would do some protesting, have some marches here in town to some of the different schools. North Junior High and Central High were two of the main schools. These were actually two of the schools that I attended as I was growing up here in Rapid. Just the tension was so high in the seventies it just seemed like it carried on from there.

The occupation of Wounded Knee went on for 73 days back in 1973. That stayed with a lot of people. While some people understood, some people didn't understand the reason for the cause for this and looked at it in a negative way. People were being arrested and being incarcerated and so there were a lot of demonstrations here in Rapid City at the different jails and even at the prison. It was a show of support for the prisoners that they weren't forgotten, that we were doing what we could to support our Indian people. Especially to support those ones who were a victim of a racist crime, or maybe a victim of an unjust sentencing.

Through this whole process Sidney would give prayer interpretation and would also give encouragement to us, that we must stand up for our children and what makes them strong makes us strong also. Also by doing this we could address this problem with racism, make people think a little bit more about what's been happening here in Rapid City. I think we as a group made a large impact into the minds of the citizens of South Dakota, they would see this on the news, on the radio, in the paper. We gave our children some encouragement and strength as they went through the discrimination in their everyday going to school. You know it might not happen to every Indian child, but it happened to enough to where we had several meetings where children would come and give testimony and air their concerns to several different groups that were working on this and some to individuals.

There was a gentleman by the name of Myron Rock. He was retired and living here in town. He was on the Rapid City Indian Health Advisory Board, but one of his real passions was to listen to these complaints. People would go over to his house and then him and his woman; they would write down any complaint and create a plan of action of how to address this complaint. The most effective way was submitting a letter to the school district or to the principle or to a teacher. He would do this a lot. I'd go over there and visit him. He'd always be addressing this and we worked on several projects together. He was handicapped but only handicapped as far as walking. Other than that he had a good heart to where he wanted to keep on. Maybe he knew his time would come and so he did the best job he could to defend our children in the school system.

I know what the prayers were and I know what the interpretation was: We had a blessing to go on with doing what we planned with the demonstrations and that it would have a negative effect to start off with, but in the end it would have a positive effect. We just had to work through the negative effect which is the first reaction that non-Indians get when they see something like this happening. They come up with their own reasons why we feel we are being treated this way. Some of them are justifiable but some aren't. You go through those stages of emotions, reactions and then you finally get down to where there's a solution, an outcome of all of this. I think the outcome was this understanding that we weren't going to accept and people shouldn't accept anything less than what anybody else is getting, or being treated. We wanted to make sure that if there was a student that was going to be kicked out that this would be on the same grounds as a non-Indian being kicked out.

One of our goals was that we might even be able to bring some native teachers into the school system, that they should start hiring more native teachers. Right now, well as of last year and I believe it's this year also; a Native American principle is at Rapid City Central High. He's in a spot where he can't show favoritism towards Native American students, but at least it shows that the administration has said 'Lets try it.' Because we do have a lot of Native American students at Central High and let's try to keep them in, let's support them. Because if a child drops out of school or a frustrated child is kicked out of school for violations, the chances are very slim after that they are going to get an education. If that's a girl she's probably going to get a teenage pregnancy or become a runaway. If it's a boy he's probably going to end up working digging ditches or doing something out there without that degree to get a good job. So we have to try to give them a chance and it's everybody's problem. Lack of an education could lead to crime, could lead into poverty, all these issues that we are going to have to deal with as a community anyhow. Our best interest is to make sure everybody gets an education that we all try to help. I think those prayers are working, we did what we could back then and I'm very proud of my involvement. Many community people spoke up and voiced their concerns and it has to be that way. Russell Means and some of the other people that came from outside of our community, they deserve to be thanked also for bringing more attention to this issue.

Twenty Three - Melvin Miner and Sidney Keith
Stories

Back in the olden days when the kids would have to come in and get ready for bed, there would be a lot of stories that the elders would tell; stories that children could learn from. Stories that deal with the creator or violence or respect or bravery. They would have a story for everything. These were all passed down and so they would tell these stories at night. That interaction was a duty that elders gladly took on. Physically they can't do all the duties of hunting and doing a lot of work, so the wisdom part of their teaching becomes more valuable. They are the ones that have all that experience from living the longest. So that became a very important duty. Also we figured that the prayers coming from elders would be more powerful, for they have been around a long time. They have this relationship with the environment and the spiritual world, so the Great Spirit or the Spirits, these helpers would listen to that and so that was a big duty. Today, how many of our people sit down with our children and tell them these stories? There are some and grandkids and children are going to benefit a lot from that. But that's something that we've lost to where that was something that probably took place every evening.

Men would tell a lot of war stories. They were in this battle or talk about a chief, a brave warrior or a real good hunter. All these stories, both the boys and girls, they would both listen to these so they would understand the different roles. So the role of the young boy is that they want you to start learning respect, as a young child, for everybody; their sister, mother, grandparents, their relatives, other people. Always being told how to treat these people when they came to visit you. What to say. What not to say. Always helping, trying to behave. Always for a boy: running, looking, being observant of wildlife, the weather, the horses, the dogs. Always keeping an open mind, watching, asking questions. Trying to learn about the environment around them. And of course, spirituality.

So a lot of times they would say, 'I wasn't to grow up to be a good person. I was to grow up to be a good father, a good man, a good hunter, a good warrior. Maybe a chief, maybe a historian. Maybe a Medicine Man, a spiritual leader. These were the options, maybe a handful of these are the main things you would shoot for in your life.

When you are growing up, especially in the years when there was more fighting with your enemies, it was like growing up in a military society. You definitely had to know how to defend yourself with other hostile tribes. Also the environment is hostile, you have to be aware, you have to learn things, survival skills.

For the girl one of those virtues is to be industrious, to make things. So she learned the customs, traditions of her people. How to be a good mother, a good wife, a good member of the camp, of the tribe itself, in this case the Lakota's. How to take care of children. So her role was, I say, limited, but her role was planned out for her. This was a good life and people accepted their roles, these were these virtues.

I remember, Joe Rockboy actually gave a talk about this and these could change a little bit. But these virtues; bravery, fortitude, generosity and wisdom, they might change a few of the words but its pretty close. Joe Rockboy had a relative called Stoneboy. Joes name is Rockboy but Stoneboy is the one they tell a story about. The Spirits told him to swallow a stone.

That by swallowing this sacred stone (it's probably pretty small) that later on in his life, not only was he going to be physically strong, but he was gonna do something good, great for our people. He's given credit with making the first bow and arrow for our people. So this Joe Rockboy came from our history and a lot of people think this is a story that we are making up but these stories are true. He's an example of a living person whose relative made this first bow. It could have been for the Lakota, Dakota, Nakota or just for his tribe but generally it's for everybody. He made the first bow, so we have these ages of how we separate the time frames through events.

Sidney Keith Makes a Whoopee Cushion

This is what I'm talking about: *tasusu*, testicle (buffalo scrotum). You take that out and it's around, it's about this big (gesturing with cupped hands) and you blow in it. Take all the outside (loose tissue), you can just tear those off. It's got a little hole in it, it's about that large (indicating the end of his little finger) you can blow in it. You can hold it together, it sticks together. The outside is dry. We used to take that and the sister-in-law would be visiting (laughing) and sit down. We'd just wait there and just before she sits down, lay that under there. She'll sit down and (the sound of air exploding through moistened lips) really embarrassing (laughing). We always used to do that. That's what its good for, to make a fart.

My mother used to be visiting a cousin and we used to carry that in there. Running Bear would say something…fart, you know. My mother would say something…fart and she really gets mad.

Not too long ago my brother was butchering. I went up to visit him and they were butchering a bull. So I butchered him and I cut the nuts off and brought 'em back. So I fixed it up, with water and all, made it stick down. When my wife goes to the door, I go behind it… fart, fart, fart and she really gets mad, (laughing)… she made me throw it away (laughing louder).

Long time ago, there's a legend. *Iktomi* was always fooling people and he fooled the Spirits too. He goes around fooling people by: "Do this," and "Do that:" and when they do it, well, it's something else. So these people said, "Let's fool this *Iktomi*." So they said, "Let's go!" So they're walking down along the creek with *Iktomi* and they seen some *onjinjintka* (rose hips). They started eating it and they said to

Iktomi, "Go ahead and eat some. It's good for you." So they just ate a few and they spit out the inside, the seeds so they quit after so many. They knew that if you eat so many, you start itching. But *Iktomi* was greedy, so *Iktomi* just kept eating, but they didn't say anything, so he got curled up right here (indicating the anus). So they started walking away. Pretty soon they looked around and he was rubbing himself. After a while he was walking and wiggling. Pretty soon, he'd stick his hand down and scratch. After a while he was using a stick, he put a stick in and he'd sit down and wiggle around. Pretty soon he took one of those (indicating a thorny stem from the *onjinjintka*) they're pretty sharp. So he'd stick himself and really let go (laughing indicating that *Iktomi* jumped a long way). His butt was all raw. That was the end of the story. That was the way they fooled him.

The same way with this *mastinca pute* (rabbits lip). You don't want to eat too much of it, your upper lip will swell up. You look like a rabbit. So *Iktomi* ate a lot of them and he was like that, his upper lip was all swollen. So they said: "Hey, *Mastinca Pute*!" they called him *Mastinca Pute*. So that's why they call the plant *mastinca pute*.

A Common Man

Iktomi was always trying to fool people. There are a lot of stories that I can't remember all of them. One was *pangi,* the beets, the wild beets. If you eat a lot of those you will fart. They told him, "Hey, eat some more of those beets." He ate them raw, you know, they're supposed to be cooked (chuckling). He ate a bunch raw. They had to go home. So, he was sitting there eating some, it works on you right away, so he was about ready, he wanted to get up. The minute he got up, fart, you know. And he took a step, fart. He just kept going. He looked back, he really looked at 'em *rude,* as if *they* were doing it, you know? (Laughing). Pretty soon, he turned around and fart, it was getting' louder and louder. He jumped up and landed and fart, he was having a hell of a time. Pretty soon, every few seconds Fart (much louder), *really* coming out, embarrassing, you know? He was goin' a long way now and well he had a little tree, he was really hanging on and his butt was just goin' (laughing, indicating that *Iktomi* was having a hard time keeping his feet on the ground). He had the fart-itis. (Laughing) So they tell us, you know, not to eat too much of this, or we'll fart.

There are a lot of those stories about each plant. Nobody bothers to remember. After a while, why, the old people quit telling it to the younger generations.

There's *Iktomi*! (Here Mr. Keith noticed a spider crawling across the floor, about ten feet away and immediately went over and stomped on it several times.) You should always say: "*Tunkashila, Wakinyan ikte!*" (Grandfather, you were killed by the Thunders!)" Those are the only ones that can kill them, the *Wankinyan*. With any little bug, you may say it that way, "They" killed them: "*Tunkashila, Wankinyan ikte.*"

Twenty Four - Melvin Miner
Holding the Sacred Pipe

One time I went to help Sidney with a ceremony, this was in Pleasant Valley up in the Black Hills, about halfway between Rapid City and Sturgis. We were inside the sweat lodge and he sent his eagle to fly over Lakota Homes our Indian community in Rapid City, a large portion of Indian people lives there. The eagle came back and said that he flew over and he saw very few people holding on to the sacred pipe with both hands. He saw more people holding on to the sacred pipe with one hand. He saw some people holding on to the sacred pipe with one hand and the Bible with the other. He saw some people, sadly to say, holding on to the sacred pipe with one hand or holding on to the Bible with one hand and holding alcohol in the other hand. And he saw people who were holding on to alcohol with both hands. The eagle reported it and he asked us that were in there to determine who we are. Which one are *you*? Which way do *you* want to live? That was the question that was asked of the ones that were in the sweat lodge.

So today we have very few that can hold the sacred pipe with both hands. Meaning you have to walk it, you have to talk it. You have to live pretty much like our ancestors lived. It's pretty hard to do today and there might be a few who are doing that. But he wanted to let us know that, to reach into our mind, our heart, to look at ourselves and determine where we stand as individuals and hopefully make an evaluation and try to make ourselves better and see if we could ever get to the point where we could hold it with two hands. One thing I know is that it would be difficult to live like our ancestors before us as far as the teaching of the pipe, the teaching of its ways. It would take someone very special to do that. There might be somebody out there.

Just about every book that I've seen brought into classrooms where there are non-Indians teaching states that there are different theories of where we came from. We came over the Bering Strait, possibly from North Carolina or somewhere out east. Somehow we made our way to Minnesota. Somewhere there in the fifteen or sixteen hundreds we were driven this way to the Dakotas and we ended up in this area. For us Natives, especially the Lakota's, we understand that we have a creation story.

A Common Man

According to the elders and our medicine people, the creation story goes like this. We come from the stars, what's out there in the universe, we came from there. So we are called the Star People, the Star Nation. We were created from the stars and we came as a Spirit nation into *He Sapa* or the Black Hills. The Star People would be *Wicahpi Oyate* and then we went into *He Sapa* into Wind Cave. We were in Wind Cave as a Spirit or semi-divine people and our instructions were to live there. As Spirits we didn't need food, we didn't need water. We saw each other through the darkness, we could see each other. We knew what was going on and over a very long time we say that *Iktomi* came to the entrance of Wind Cave. The spider is a trickster, but he also has many other qualities, so this animal convinced us, convinced our people to emerge, telling us how beautiful it was out in his world. So we went ahead and made the decision to emerge and see all this beauty. Then we were born just like a woman gives birth. In emerging we soon found out that we're not semi-divine any more but we're human. We need clothing. We need to take care of ourselves. We need food and so we gather a lot of the plant life that's available to us.

Eventually we strike up a deal with the buffalo nation. The pact that we have with them is they will provide their body for us and they will provide almost everything we need with food, shelter, clothing and tools and we'll be taken care of this way. So we lived that way a long time and eventually our people multiplied and we moved out east. But my point is that we come to this conclusion through oral history and through ceremonies.

    Over time this is where the dialects are born. So we have Lakota, Dakota, Nakota and what comes from there are the seven main divisions and what is commonly known as the seven council fires. It's a title we have and one of several. There are four tribes that make up the Dakota dialect which is located pretty close to what is known as Spirit or Knife Lake in Minnesota. The Dakota dialect is associated more with our people who ventured into the Minnesota region. And then two other divisions, Yankton and Yanktonians, those are the ones that lived in between the four that live in Minnesota. They would speak the Nakota dialect. Then the Teton Lakota that live out here around the Black Hills would speak the Lakota dialect and this would be the Oglala, Hunkpapa,

Minneconjou and the Brule. Then we also have the Two Kettle and we have the Blackfeet and we have the Sans Arc.

If there is something we would like to know about that happened in the past, we take it to a ceremony or to a spiritual man who works with the Spirits and he would give us an answer in the ceremony. This answer might not be the answer non-Indians would like to hear, or archaeologists or historians. But this is the answer that the Spirits give us, for this is how we gain a lot of our history. This is how we retain the stories that go back hundreds of thousands of years to even go a step further to the creation of this earth, which no person was alive at that time, only the Great Spirit. Yet all of our ceremonies incorporate everything, all of the universe.

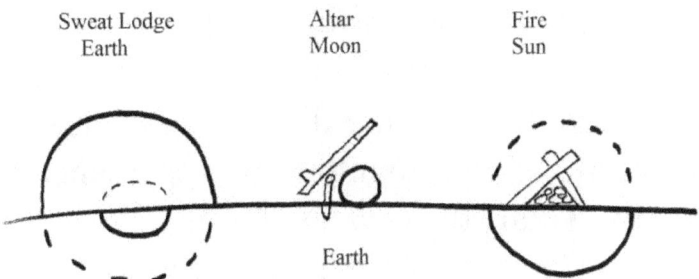

Let's use the sweat lodge for example. We have the sweat lodge made out of willows in a dome shape, these willows are bent and placed into the earth and they are covered (a long time ago) with buffalo hide. In the middle of that sweat lodge, there's dirt that's removed that represents the outer layer, the crust of the earth. That crust of the earth is six inches down or it's a foot down, it depends on how deep you want to dig this pit. The sweat lodge is facing the west direction (it could be facing the west or the east) and you would place that pit dirt and make a mound not too far away from the entrance of the sweat that could be three feet could be four feet. This is an altar where a buffalo skull or a rack to hold the sacred pipe is placed. Then if you go out further, another six to ten feet, there would be a pit. That would be a fire pit for heating up the stones. Once those are heated up, then those are brought into the sweat lodge, walking counter- clockwise and those are placed inside the pit inside the sweat lodge.

    Now on the spiritual description, the fire pit would represent the Sun. The mound that we made from the dirt from the crust of the earth is put together to represent the Moon. Then the sweat lodge represents Mother Earth and the pit will represent the center of the Earth. We have knowledge of this and we're recreating the creation through this ceremony. There's a lot of symbolism in this, with this buffalo skull, this sun, the sun light. Wisdom works through this buffalo skull which represents a buffalo, to teach us ceremonies, but mainly to teach us the Sun Dance. This is what gives us life; the sun and the buffalo give us life, wisdom and strength. So we know that these are part of the Great Spirit.

Inside the sweat lodge, the heat is there, this is how the Earth was born, matured; through a lot of heat. We have some sort of water container there and the water, which we as Native Americans say is our first medicine, water can cure most things. When the door is closed we'll take a buffalo horn, just like a long time ago, dip it in and then we'll pour this water on these heated rocks, just like the old days. It produces this steam that we call the breath of the Great Spirit. These rocks represent the *Tunkashilas* or the grandfathers of this world. The rocks are the oldest so they represent the grandfathers. They have a Spirit and so when we pour this water on there it produces this steam, this heat that takes out the impurities from our bodies. At the same time it's a sacred time, it's a sacred steam that we breathe in. We take a fresh breath, something that's given from the rocks and the water combined and we're trying to cleanse our self through this.

There was a time when everything was dark, there was darkness before the sun was made. Even as it's dark inside and we're going through this creation ceremony, the spirituality follows this creation story. Bit by bit, inch by inch, year by year we are living with the Spirits. We've grown up with them from the time we left Wind Cave, even before that we could see the wonder of the creation working. This is what the ceremony is about. The prayers that we give in there are to thank this creation: so we give thanks. We realize that there are four directions, four winds of this Earth and we give thanks. We acknowledge them as separate entities. We acknowledge the Great Spirit or the sky and then we acknowledge Mother Earth as these are the first creations. We've been doing these ceremonies for thousands of years. This is what we have learned; this is what we were taught. The ceremony has a relationship to the creation of this world. Every ceremony has a relationship to the creation and also to the entities of this world. So what we practice we can see more and more through scientists, their findings are starting to coincide with what we already know. Not in detail but in a practical way, of how the moon was made, how the sun was made and how they play a major part in our existence. It has a meaning to it, it has a spiritual meaning that comes with it and so we know it is sacred. The Medicine Man that is inside the ceremony, he will be working with the Spirits and those Spirits will interpretate to him. Either they want us to know something or we will ask the spiritual leader for an answer to a question. This is where we find wisdom, through the sweat lodge, for they will tell us a secret about the universe, how it was made, what its function- its purpose is and how does that relate to us as in this case as Lakota people. To even go beyond that they will tell us things that are going to happen in the future. That could be a prophecy or they could just tell us something on a smaller scale, something that will affect the world or a people or it could just affect our self or our family. But this is how we gain the knowledge, through all of these ceremonies that we conduct, the sweat lodge being one of them, the sacred pipe of just praying, the *hanbleceya* ceremony, the Sun Dance ceremony, the *hunkapi* making of relatives ceremony, the becoming of a woman ceremony and the throwing of the ball or the keeping of the soul ceremony. Sometimes they call praying with the pipe a separate ceremony or it just goes with all the rest of the ceremonies so it could be seven or it could be eight ceremonies.

Somebody might say how do you know? Of course it's not written down, so how do we know this is true? We say simply: We have Spirits that work with the Great Spirit, God and we communicate with them. We've proven ourselves through the time of history to be a good people and to be given that ability to work with the Spirits. Not all of us but a small percentage that interpretate what the Spirits say. So things that we need to know will be passed on to us and then we must pass those on further. That's where Sidney Keith, like this book, reached a lot of people, hundreds maybe thousands of people through his life. And his life in a spiritual sense where he obtained this power, didn't really begin, he told me, until he was fifty years old. So he didn't spend all of his life in dealing with this responsibility as a Medicine Man or a spiritual leader or as an interpreter. So by doing this book and describing some of the events that took place, some of the stories some of the people would call miracles, we would just call spiritual happenings, can be shared in a way with people who are interested in learning more about our culture. That spirituality - it's not dead. It still goes on. This is a gift that we're giving as a people and a gift that he was given and through his twenty seven years of spiritually helping people. He has made a big difference and can be used as an example, a teacher to our people, to other tribes, to other nations. That we can obtain through prayer an understanding of this world, an understanding of where we fit in as human beings and where the Spirits fit in, what their duties, their responsibilities are. I think we will see that we are very close to other religions and how we conduct our spiritual lifestyle.

It seems like a lot of our ceremonies dealt with our relationship with and our knowledge of nature and how we have utilized nature through a respect that we have for nature. Just to give you an example of that respect you know we were gatherers, we were hunters, we were a mobile people, you might say nomads. We followed the buffalo herds and we would also follow sacred places. We would have to be at this sacred place at this certain time of the year then we would have to be at this next sacred place or at a safe place. So we did a lot of traveling and there's always exceptions to this, but in the history of our people, we don't know of any family or and any individuals that said, "You know what? I like this little piece of land by the Black Hills. I want to stay here and live here. This one spot." It was unheard of. Yes it is beautiful and it would be sacred and this we would enjoy for the moment, but we must move on. There are other places to go and so individual ownership of the land is something that we did not practice. We realized that we are not here to own anything, but we are here as caretakers. We took care of the land and we tried to balance out the wildlife. Taking what we needed and not over killing, not having a camp in one area for too long in one area for it would scar the land. This land had a great abundance of resources.

    Everything has a reason and a right to be where it's at. We respected that and we knew that we were the last to be put on earth, so we're the visitor to this land. We must respect that and we understood that. We have a respect for the land, the four legged, the winged, the water creatures, the green relatives or the root relatives. The Great Spirit taught us that respect. As we practiced that, we gained more wisdom. We gained more blessings from the Great Spirit, so we behold many blessings. One of them is to have the Spirits directly talk to our spiritual leaders and then we can talk back. It's the communication, they can talk to us and we can talk back. Some people have the ability to hear Spirits, but they can't talk to them. Some people can talk to Spirits, but the Spirits won't talk to them. They will show them things, they will help them and a lot of us have that ability. We can speak to the Spirits or to God and he will help us, but he just won't speak to us in a language that we can hear. But we know that the Spirit is there protecting us or watching over us or providing some comfort and guidance to us.

Most of us have that ability to speak to the Spirits and some of us cultivate that into something more too where we can start to hear things or like in our case the Lakota, we can hear the Spirits and communicate with them. Also when we go to sleep we can dream and we believe the Spirits work through our dreams to us and what we see in a dream will come true. Through this happening over and over and over again through years it gives validation to this gift that we have and we exercise that gift with belief. We know this has happened for thousands and thousands of years. We have dreams that we visit places that we talk to people, things happen. We see events happening and this is a big part of our spirituality. So even in our sleep we are spiritually active. A certain group of our people are called elk dreamers and they have the ability more than any other dreamers that we have in the other societies that they will dream of something on a steady basis. They could do this every night, every other night as needed.

So in the daytime and as we sleep, we have the spirituality working for us. Our Spirits are working to guide us, to give us strength, to give us wisdom and we just have to be aware of that. This might help if it happens to other cultures, to other Indian tribes, to other people throughout the world. I just know that this happens to us on a steady basis. This is not far fetched or something that somebody might say I've heard of our people doing. It goes on today and a good example of that I have spoken about was Joe Rockboy and that he told me he was an elk dreamer. Back in Vermillion, in college Joe Rockboy had several dreams about me and he came to me to speak to me about them. He wanted me to quit drinking and he said that he wanted me also at the same time to help the people more in a leadership role. He told me some things that only I knew. He told me that he was not told this; it was relayed to him in a dream. He said, "My dreams are real. I'm going to come to give you some warning about something that's going to happen and I'm going to tell you about something that did happen. Then I'm going to ask you for a favor." He wanted me to put on a Pow Wow and that the Spirits asked for this. So I said I would go ahead and try my best. Of course in college I was having fun, too much fun. He put some seriousness into my life. So I ended up helping put on several Pow Wows down in Vermillion. We had Joe as the announcer at one of them and this was to honor him for actually making this Pow Wow happen. This is where I seen a prayer that he gave when he wanted this Pow Wow to happen and we also prayed for this and so I seen some of how it works. There's a protocol into getting things done, especially when it involves the people.

There are a few books out now from like the Sinte Gleska College and maybe from Oglala Lakota College that agree that we came from the Black Hills, but the academic community will not acknowledge or support this idea. But this is how we are going to do it and it will come out in a good way on this for I've been at too many ceremonies that support this. This is why we hold this place sacred, the Black Hills. This is why we call it our birthplace and why it will always be connected to us. We will never sell it and someday part of it will be returned to us. Actually when that happens the spirituality that we already have will increase and the reason why is there are Spirits that stay at these sacred places like Bear Butte, Devil's Tower and the Black Hills and they watch over the sacred places for us.

Our tribe covered a wide range of area going into what is now North Dakota, Nebraska, a little bit of Montana and this area right west of the Black Hills, the Powder River area. These areas separating the Black Hills from different tribes, these were kind of buffer zones, anybody can go in there, but there was usually a lot of fighting if two tribes ran into each other. That's probably where they would run into each other, right on the borders. The landscape would determine the borders of where you could go and where you couldn't go. So our people traveled all the way down to the middle part of Nebraska and then in a big circle going all the way over to Minnesota and then coming all the way around again. It was a good strategy to have our people located on the perimeter of the area that we wanted to keep. Mainly not just for land reasons but for enough wild game. There was buffalo but also you need to get something else in your diet and that would be antelope and deer.

The sacred places that we have within this area would be the Black Hills, Devils Tower (which we call Grey Horn Butte), Bear Butte and then all the way across over to Pipestone, Minnesota where you can get the sacred pipestone. It was important that we protect the sacred site which contained the pipestone, so that was crucial for us to control that. Also the Black Hills had a lot of the medicine, the herbs and plants and sacred places within the Black Hills, it was important for us to control that area. The problem with Devils Tower and Bear Butte is that several tribes on our western border also wanted to lay claim to that area. So it was something that we had access to but we might have to fight for that right to utilize that spirituality, for there were several tribes that had an interest in protecting that.

Standing Up Bull was the first camp chief. He was from what they call Itazipa (the French called them Sans Arc) and the interpretation is without bows, like bows and arrows. They had bows that weren't made very good because of the material that they used or they didn't have very good bow makers, one of those two. But they were a kind of pitiful band. The Great Spirit, looking at our people at that time gave the Sacred Buffalo Calf Pipe to the poorest band and Standing Up Buffalo was the chief of that band. The rules, the laws came with the Sacred Pipe were told at this time. It's kind of like the 10 Commandments and that was kind of our Ark.

    The Sacred Pipe came so we had to protect it. My theory is and I would think that a lot of people would agree with me on this, is that this band traveled within the center of our vast land. We had other bands protecting the border and this band would be in the middle, being protected. They stayed on the west side of the Missouri River that runs right down the middle of South Dakota. So this band could have access if they wanted to the Black Hills, Bear Butte, Devils Tower, these sacred places and the Badlands. They would be protected along all four sides so that they could keep this sacred pipe protected. So it stayed that way and it stayed an open secret in the sense that other tribes knew about it because they would hear about us getting this Big Medicine, this Sacred Pipe that came in a sacred way. Some of our people would tell our allies, like the Cheyenne people and they also had sacred items, gifts, brought to them by the Great Spirit. So for awhile their people would hear about the many blessings, the power that we had. They would call us The Pipe People. So instead of calling us Lakota, Nakota or Dakota, they would say, "They're The Pipe People. They are the ones with the Sacred Pipe." So we were known as that for some time.

I believe the strategy from that pipe time was to protect it within the boundaries of our area and try to centrally locate it. This idea or this strategy is very similar to the buffalo herds, that if there was a white buffalo it seemed like that white buffalo was in the middle of the herd. It was being protected by the herd. It was very hard to get to. We are talking about herds that have thousands and thousands that would be around this white buffalo. Every now and then a white buffalo would be taken from that herd and quite to my astonishment: it was an honor to go out and see if you could kill the white buffalo. I think the reasoning to that is if you didn't do it as a Lakota, another tribe would do it and maybe it would be an enemy tribe and they would gain the healing and spiritual powers from that white buffalo. So you felt it was your duty to do this and also by doing this you would not be condemned, but you would use this white buffalo hide and the skull in some ceremonies or what they would call the a ghost lodge, where they would keep this white buffalo hide after they tanned it. If somebody was sick or somebody wanted to do something spiritually, they would go in that tipi or that lodge where the hide was and sit on there and pray. The Medicine Man would use this to heal people. The owner of it would be given a blessing to help heal people. I know in the Big Missouri Winter Count that has 131 symbols representing each year, there are seven references to the white buffalo. There were also descriptions that the white buffalo's were faster than regular buffalo and were harder to obtain because they were protected by the other buffalo. So it was very hard to obtain this but once you did you could use it for spiritual reasons so that was the good thing about it.

    There is a story told that at the direction of the superintendent of Cheyenne River and the council they went and confiscated the Sacred Pipe and they took a picture of it. Four police officers: the ones that were involved in taking this, all died. There's something to be said about that, the protection of where the Pipe should be. Nobody should ever try to steal it or take it, it protects itself. Some people might think they have a claim to it or they want it moved to their reservation, but because of what took place they won't try to take it. The four police officers who were innocent, they were doing their job, it didn't matter, the sacredness is above that law or that order that was given for it's taking. A picture was taken of the Sacred Pipe and the superintendent thought twice after these things were happening so they returned the Sacred Pipe. Then he remembered he had a picture, so he gave it to my father-in-law, Sidney. When he was telling me the story, he said, "I had it here for a long time. I put it in a certain book. I looked at it several times, wondering what to do with it. As far as we ever know, that was the only picture ever taken of it. After a time, I went into that book one day and I opened it up. That picture was gone. It just vanished. So all this time I was wondering, what am I going to do with it? The Spirits went ahead and just took it, which is the best thing for that."

An area that we shared with other tribes was the sacred pipestone quarries up in Pipestone, Minnesota. That location was a place that we had an interest in and not denying other tribes there was an unwritten rule. We protected the sacred site, but we could trade for it if they wanted to. What we believe is that this pipe was given to our people, that we are the keeper and the teachers of the use of this pipe, but other tribes could, if they wanted to adopt this belief they could. All that they had to have was a good heart and a good mind. So we could trade them this pipestone and we could work with them to teach them this way of understanding which was very easy for these other tribes to do. We treated the environment the same. We also believed that there was a supreme being who made everything. We believed that there are Spirits that were made by the Great Spirit as helpers, angels. Also when we came into existence that man, by dying, developed a Spirit. So it could be a Spirit made by the Great Spirit this way in the creation or a Spirit could come from us as humans. So the first Spirits are older, then the animal Spirits are next and then us. So like I said, we are the last to come onto Mother Earth. We could trade this pipestone and we'd also learn from other tribes about their way of thinking; about their way of praying. So we had spirituality pretty much the same as other tribes' belief system, but we are all given a creation separately from each other. So this we respected but this is also what divided us or gave us our uniqueness. We know that Lakota's came from the Black Hills, other tribes have their own creation stories on where they came from.

In the beginning we didn't know about the red pipestone, we knew of a black pipestone in Northern South Dakota by the Rosebud Reservation. We found out that you can carve the red pipestone for these pipes fairly easily. They're softer than most stones, yet hard enough and you can heat them without them breaking and that was really the combination that you need. This is something that was hard yet easy to carve and yet that could hold heat and not crack it or break it. The pipestone, called Catlinite which is named after a non-Indian who visited the quarry so somebody gave it that name. This began when the Sacred Pipe came and these estimates go from 700 to 1000 years ago.

The black pipestone was what we were more familiar with at first. It's kind of grey as you find it, but as you polish it up it turns into a black. It's like the buffalo horns; they're kind of black yet if you really look they have a grayish tint to it, because of the weather on the outside layer, but as you polish it up you can get a real shiny black. That's how this pipestone is. So this black pipestone, you can use it to pray with. There are a couple of differences and they probably evolved throughout the years, depending on what type of spiritual leader or Medicine Man you are. If you are a spiritual leader that would work with the west direction there's a good chance you would have a black pipestone pipe to pray with, to use for ceremonies. Also I've heard that in times of war sometimes they would use the black pipestone pipe to take to different tribes and smoke, asking within our selves, our own nation to support this battle, this war and then to neighboring tribes that were allies to us to help us fight the enemy. So these are two reasons that are different than regular pipestone.

Let's talk about a little bit different leadership roles. There would have been a camp leader, one who deals with the activities of the camp: the decision making: when to move onto another campsite: the best way that they could protect themselves in the landscape that they're at. He would make these decisions kind of like the mayor today in the cities.

A long time ago we had a spiritual leader in a camp to maintain certain entities that you need to make up a healthy functioning powerful band. This band could be made up of 20 people all the way up to 100 people. He's the one that would conduct the religious ceremonies. He would have that vision or that know-how on dealing with anything that was sacred. He would be there to explain it. He would deal with the healing of people who got sick in some type of way. The term Medicine Man probably comes more from the era where they relied on roots and plants more than we do today. Even as spiritual leaders a lot of spiritual leaders will have some know-how in some use of herbs, but nothing compared to what the Medicine Man or Medicine Woman would have in the past. They would know literally hundreds of herbs and like I said, the Black Hills is where probably a majority of those herbs are located. Not only is it a spiritual island but also it's a place that has our sacred plants, so that we can use them in healing.

Then you would have had an historian and that could be the chief, that could be the spiritual leader or that could be somebody different. The historian could be an artist such as the one who would record events or interpretate events. He could be the keeper of the winter count, the painted hide that would be a written record of the tribe. One symbol represents one year. This could be passed down to him or he could start a whole new winter count. A lot of these winter counts go between 50 years and 150 years, so of course the ones that are over 50 years are probably passed on to a relative or somebody who showed a skill or an interest in being that winter count keeper. We would have somebody there who would keep this account going.

Then you would have a war chief. Somebody who's demonstrated their ability in battle that you would trust their judgment and you would be willing to follow them into battle. Someone who had natural leadership or strategic ability, so that's what you would look for, I mean besides bravery and the skill level of him as a warrior. A good war chief would take you into battle and bring you back out alive. So you would pick that person that was the most qualified, just like the camp chief would have the ability to make good decisions for the job that he was chosen to do. He could be removed at any time. They're not elected for life, they're appointed by the people. Let's say there was a hunting party. There might be a chief or a leader for that hunting party and he might be different from the rest. If he goes out and makes some bad decisions, comes back with no game, maybe the next day or the next week they say we're going to follow somebody else and that person has to abide to that. Then he becomes a follower or a participant until he proves himself again. Then he can move into that position again so it could also happen with the camp leader.

The only one that I would feel had a somewhat permanent position would be the spiritual leader, since he was selected not by the people but by the Great Spirit. He is given a spiritual job and we can't take that away from him, his abilities, but the Spirits can. A lot of times he has to do things more strictly, more controlling than we have to. He has to live a certain way. He has to speak a certain way. He has to perform his job, his spiritual job in a certain way. He has Spirits to help him, but if he doesn't, then people say that's between him and the Great Spirit, that's not between us and him. So his job could last all of his life if he does it right. Sometimes we can't interfere as the people. We could voice our concerns and we don't have to follow him, but the Great

Spirit is the only one that can take his powers away.

We have the four ages: the Rock Age. That's where we honor the Rock; we say that was here first. The Great Spirit gave everything that he had and then became a rock. But he still has all that ability, that authority. Then all the other entities and we have sixteen major entities that we think that the world is made up of. The sixteen are the main entities like the sun and the moon, the earth; the four winds are part of those entities. There are sixteen of them, then there are sub-entities under those, the four main ones there's sub-entities underneath those. So that there are sixteen in all that we really recognize and it's called the sixteen or the four by four. Somebody might be praying and they'll say by the four by four and we know what that is. They covered sixteen entities and so like the tipi, the average tipi would have sixteen poles. As a teacher, a grandmother or father, they can have one pole represent one of those entities. They can teach their children inside the tipi, especially in the winter time. This first pole represents the Sun and tells about that creation. The second pole represents the Earth and can tell about the Earth and then the Moon and then the four winds and so on and so forth. They understand that, they see it, they visualize it and in the sweat lodge the same way. Sixteen willows are used to make that sweat lodge. It's not a very big sweat lodge, that's a sweat lodge that if they used the sixteen, that it would represent those sixteen powers, those sixteen ribs of a buffalo. So it has a lot of meaning to it, the sixteen.

We had the Rock Age and then the Fire Age and then the Bow and Arrow Age and then the Pipe Age. Now if there was another age, that would make a fifth age, it definitely would be the Horse Age. The horse made that much of an impact on our people in a positive way.

Let's say they decide to move camp and the reasons are many: they are following the buffalo; the herds maybe moved on several miles. Maybe there are some enemies close by and they want to move: their camp site has been spotted. Maybe there's bad weather coming. They're looking for a better location. You always want a safe location, a location that has plenty of firewood, plenty of water, protection. So these places were well known a long time ago, so they would know about these places. But the weather is the part that is unpredictable. Snowfall could come early, rains could come early, flash floods could come. Things like this. Buffalo could move out of the area, so then you would have to travel long distances. Before the horse, you had to be on top of everything. Decisions had to be made quickly, especially when it came to food. If you were on foot, you had to have scouts, messengers going from band to band, informing each other of where the buffalo herds were. Even though we were talking about 30 to 60 million buffalo's out on the plains of the United States and Canada and going all the way down to Texas, all the way over to the Mississippi and all the way over to the Rockies. Still these herds can be gone for several days or weeks, so you have to track them down. Some days they are plentiful, some days they are scarce. Before the horse it was essential that you constantly had scouts or trackers tracking these herds down and reporting back to the camp. Then your camp was more on the move. But after the horse, then it became a lot easier, you could travel a great distance to do a buffalo hunt and then carry the meat back. So the horse made it a lot easier, especially if you miscalculated on some calculations there. It could make up the difference there the distance and the time with the horse.

When we received the Sacred Pipe, life changed spiritually. It put a focus on our full creation. It took us thousands and thousands of years to get to that point of understanding this creation. So the Great Spirit rewarded us with the Sacred Pipe to continue on in a spiritual way. Life got better, it got more spiritual, we gained more understanding of what was coming. We were rising consciously to a new level of relationship with the Great Spirit and with everything else. We realized the Great Spirit was everything. It seems like that era was short lived for we know that there were European people that would come into this area before the 1800's. We'd have a few here, a few there but really after 1800 more and more Europeans started coming in. I would say the golden years were from the time that we did receive the Sacred Pipe up until the 1800's.

Twenty Five - Melvin Miner
Pipe Protocol

A long time ago it would be that you would present your filled pipe to a Medicine Man. Well today they have a thing called *chungliska,* it's tobacco, s*ka* is white, like white man tobacco cigarette or cigarettes come in the white papers, the white tobacco, it can mean either one. Today we're still supposed to be practicing this also and probably half the time I offer a pipe and half the time I offer a cigarette, so I do it both ways. You could bring a cigarette or a pipe and present this: you still turn around in front of him and then you have to do the four times with the pipe. By doing that you would recognize the six directions, what they would call *dako wakan* or that that is holy or that that has a Spirit. So you're involving everything that has a Spirit into your prayer and this prayer is sent out by doing this with your pipe. Then you would take this pipe and you would go to the individual. By him seeing you with this pipe, he knows that there is going to be something sacred going on. Most times with the pipe you're either giving a *wopila,* because something good happened, somebody got well or some situation turned out good or that there is something of a problem and so you want the Medicine Man to pray or to interpretate something. So you approach the individual. You stop in front of him and you turn counter-clockwise. Then you tell him that you want to offer him this Sacred Pipe. He puts his hands out in front of him. You take your pipe and you put it forward and then you bring it back, forward and back, forward and back forward four times. If his hands are out there the forth time you lay the pipe in his hands. You have to remember the pipe bowl is in your left hand and he will take the pipe, accept it.

There are cases where a Medicine Man might not accept it. He could just put his hands up and say, "No. I can't." for whatever reason. Or he can take it in his hands and then he could remove the stem from the bowl and say, "I can't accept this" and maybe give a reason why. Rarely have I seen that done. But if he accepts it you'll talk with him and then when it's done he'll give a prayer. Then you will both smoke it or ever who's around there might share in the pipe. If somebody does smoke it with you they might go ahead and give a prayer, a silent prayer or you can speak out loud.

So they might hold it for awhile, pray and then light it, smoke it. They might even burn some sage at that time or when the Medicine Man is speaking with the person. Sage, sweetgrass, cedar, these are all used when there is a sacred moment, sacred event, sacred dance, something sacred going on. The smoke or the smell from this smoke protects the sacred event that is going on. It also prevents the negative, negative Spirits, negative things from coming into that ceremony. So it protects it and at the same time it summons. Some of the Spirits smell it. They know that there is something sacred there so they want to come and help, to listen, see if they can help. So it benefits the ceremony when sage, sweetgrass, cedar is burnt at that time. So a lot of people will smudge their house, maybe everyday, maybe every other day. Hoping for protection, knowing that it will help them keep their health, their house cleansed from anything negative.

The four times with the pipe actually allows both parties, the one presenting the pipe and the one who receives the pipe to think four times if they want to do this. Sometimes you might, lets say you might want to quit drinking or you might want to go up on the hill or you might want to Sun

Dance, you know, something tough. During those four times, you have to think if you really want to do this. At the same time, the Medicine Man, especially if he knows what you are going to do, he's allowed that same opportunity. He might say, "I don't want to accept this pipe. For I don't think you are ready for what you are going to ask me." Or, "I don't think this is the right time." So there's a moment in there, the four times when to change your mind, to think about it. So you can bring the cigarette to them. This is pretty much the offering or *opagi* or the offering of tobacco to engage in a spiritual conversation with a spiritual leader or Medicine Man, holy man. They will all tell you:

We're not holy. We work with the Spirits. They are the ones that are holy, but we are the interpreter. They teach us, they tell us and then we pass this on to you. Without them we can't do all these things. So our egos shouldn't be real powerful. We realize that somebody gave us this power to use for the people. They gave it to us, they could take it back. It's more powerful, more meaningful when we help people, not our self, but to help the people. We are here to help our future generations, especially when it deals with health or for a better life; especially for our future generations of our people.

So for many years, I had that luxury of when Sidney was living with us or when he was living not to far from us of engaging this interpretation. I could do that and anybody else that's around; who grew up with a Medicine Man or Medicine Woman's home has the advantage of that. One day I went to him and I was going to offer him a cigarette and he put his hands up and said, "I can't accept it." I said, "Oh, is that right?" He said, "The reason why is my Spirits all took off." And I said, "They all took off?" He said, "They informed me that there was a council with the Spirits. Mine were involved in it. They said it could take up to four days for this council." I don't know if they meet once a year or once every four years or what. But he said, "I just pray that nothing, no emergency happens, during these next four days. Because I'm kind of helpless in case there's a really bad emergency, like somebody dying or something. So I have to wait." I said, "What would you think the council is about?" He said, "It would have to be very important, major, something major. Decisions are going to be discussed and it definitely has an impact on our people and it could be several things, but I don't want to guess. But it has to be important." So that was the only time I have run into that.

Sometimes I know that somebody's Spirits will be at another ceremony, another Medicine Man's. You know they don't own that Spirit but that Spirit chooses to work with them or is assigned to them. Somebody might say well this certain kind of Spirit came into our ceremony and he has a name. It could be an animal or a bird or person or a chief. A Medicine Man could say, "Well that Spirit goes into this other Medicine Man's ceremony a lot." They realize the Spirits that are with them chose to be with them, help them. But they also might go visit another altar, another ceremony, sometimes out of respect. It's complicated to a certain degree that I don't know all the secrets to this and I probably never will. But sometimes I've heard where Spirits have said, "I've gone to that ceremony, but I stayed at a distance out of respect for that man's Spirits that help him. I stood at a distance and I watched and good things are in that ceremony. So I just prayed from a distance."

And then several times I know on issues dealing with the people as a whole and an example would be the Black Hills Treaty issue, or major Spiritual issues the Spirits will seek a higher power. I know this from different Medicine Men that I go to and this has happened before too with Sidney. Say an interpretation would be my Spirit will *opagi* the sacred Calf Pipe or go up to the Calf Pipe House and will *opagi* this Sacred Pipe, kind of a big Spirit that has a lot of power or authority, this first pipe. So they might not always give you an answer right there. They'll say we're going to go there and we'll take your prayers and your request and we'll get back with you. So that way too it could be done or they could say in so many days, four days, seven days, we'll have an answer for you. So even the Spirits sometimes takes time to answer something, it doesn't always come right away for a Medicine Man. Sometimes they have things to do on their end or sometimes the individual say such as myself is asking for something they want to watch me or they want to make sure I'm committed or capable or sincere about the request also. Sometimes, well most of the time it's all favorable. Sometimes they say not right now or next year you know so and that's what you want to know.

A long time ago they would say: if you want to know something, go to a ceremony and you will find an answer. They did that many times a long time ago. Today a lot of us still do that. If we want to know something we go to ceremony. A lot of times that's where say non-believers or people who are questioning might ask, "Well how do you guys know this for sure? Are you sure this is correct?" We will say, "We went to a ceremony. This is what our ancestors said and this is what we go by." So, some believe, some don't. But this is a real powerful gift given to us. So we work that way, live that way, think that way and believe that way.

I asked Sidney the question of how he obtained some of his Spirits. He told me about a few of his Spirits he obtained. One he said he went to a Medicine Man named Felix Green down in Cherry Creek or Red Scaffold. He said when he was done with his *hanbleceya* that a spotted eagle was one of his Spirits from Felix. So he said this Eagle helped him out, he used it quite a bit. In another ceremony (these are *hanbleceya* ceremonies) he was fasting and praying, he said this was in a sweat lodge. He said as he was sitting there praying something was moving towards him, but in kind of a nice way, a comfortable way where he wasn't frightened by it. He said that a deer laid his head on his lap and he rubbed the deer's head. The deer introduced himself; it was a black-tailed deer. Different Spirits have different qualities or healing skills and so he obtained that black-tailed deer through that *hanbleceya* in the sweat lodge.

I know he had an elk and he said that this elk appeared to him. This elk was facing him standing and he said this elk put his head down and put his racks into Mother Earth. The elk stated that *'no man, no wind, no disease can move me from this spot.'* So it's a gift, but interpretating that meaning: this elk has a history of working with medicine men, working with the leaders. It's a symbol that is associated with leadership; a lot of our great leaders have had help from the elk Spirit. In this case it could also help him heal diseases. Also, the elk is associated with relationships so a person who does have this ability to work with this elk usually is called upon to address relationship problems between people, a man and a wife or between brothers and sisters. Because we all have problems or disputes with one another so for some reason it is associated with that.

He had a red-tailed hawk that would also come into ceremonies and then also this buffalo. I don't mind talking about what kind of Spirits they work with as long as somebody has passed. But let's say my friends who practice, I would hate to talk about their Spirits without their permission, but I have seen this with other books, like Fools Crow. As long as Fools Crow is describing the Spirits of somebody else, then I think its okay on this.

Also I remember asking the father-in-law about how you can obtain these Spirits through the *hanbleceya* and he told me there were four ways. A couple of them aren't practiced today. The most common one probably 95 per cent of the people you would go up on a hill, such as Bear Butte up on the Butte, but you can also go out basically anywhere that's secluded and you would set up an altar with the help of a Medicine Man and some helpers. Then you would stay inside that altar and fast and pray and sing for between one and four days. You can go inside a sweat lodge and I have done this several times and then also stay in there and fast and pray.

Then he told me two other ways and I can see why they are difficult to do. This third way was to (and you've got to imagine this was 100's of years ago) but you would have your ceremony, your *hanbleceya* probably after a sweat lodge. You'd have your people there and you could actually walk, along with your pipe, follow a stream. It could be 50 miles and you turn back and come back that same way and ever what you seen on your journey and ever how long that took, that you come back and have that interpretated. So you can set out walking and as long as you are holding your sacred pipe you'll be protected. Also in your seeking a vision, you're going through a lot of prayers, singing songs. That could be done a long time ago; probably today it would be very difficult.

Then the forth way he told me was to *hanbleceya* in water, like a stream, of course nothing too deep I would think anyhow, but that was the forth way in which he was told. It sounds kind of dangerous in a way. I'm not sure it would work. I didn't pursue that method but I don't know anybody that's done it that way. There are exceptions. Different people in trying to obtain certain Spirits or a certain method they would also use the pit, where they would dig a pit in the ground and then *hanbleceya* inside there. Then also to the extreme might be someone wrapped up. They might hang with their feet being wrapped up hanging downwards. Which causes, I guess, the blood would flow to your head. I'm not sure how long you can withstand something like this. You might even be able to *hanbleceya* in a tree as long as you are tied there.

There are some different methods to *hanbleceya.* I've heard of a story of someone hanging from their feet in a *hanbleceya*. People do go into pits. The pits almost look like a grave and then they are covered up with a board. I mean you have air; you just want to make sure it's dark inside there. There's actually one that I've heard of being staked out. Meaning there would be four stakes, two would hold your feet and two stakes would be for your hands. You would be staked out. These are methods that you definitely need a Medicine Man and some people to participate in so that nothing goes wrong. They are very dangerous because once you make those vows to go up there, one day, two days three or four especially three or four days and you run into trouble or you get weak or you have doubt or you feel you can't complete your vision, that's where it becomes dangerous because you can't release yourself, so people have to be monitoring these *hanbleceya* ceremonies. But you are also trying to seek Spirits, trying to seek answers or you are trying to give thanks, or probably the big thing, health for yourself or your family, relatives or your people. You are praying for the generations, future generations so that they can have a better life. You are always thanking the Spirits and the ancestors for allowing this to happen; they carried it on and kept this tradition alive, this culture.

Twenty Six - Melvin Miner
The Four Ages

We call the first age of our people the Rock Age. We have the Rock Age; how the earth, the sun, the moon, everything comes from the rock. Then it goes to the Fire Age; how we could use fire for warmth, to cook with, for protection. The next age would be the Bow and Arrow Age; how the Bow and Arrow made hunting a lot easier: from just throwing a rock or trapping or spearing prey. This bow and arrow is more efficient and also in battle, the bow and arrow can be used to protect yourself or to kill the enemy. Then the last age is the Pipe Age. The Sacred Pipe; where we as a people have come to a point where we learned many things and we were given a gift of the Sacred Pipe. It put everything in perspective; we can see the full picture now. How we can address the universe, the four directions, mother earth, the sky. We can address everything and have a better understanding of how we relate and where we stand within this creation. By receiving that pipe we became a better person or a better tribe with a better understanding. So there are our four ages as we have broken it down to.

So this Bow and Arrow Age, this Stoneboy comes from that. Joe Rockboy gave this speech at a workshop, he mentioned bravery and I've also heard this from other medicine men. Bravery is the first step for anybody to do anything. A person must have this bravery to accept responsibility or to take a challenge or to take a first step. Even as a child learning how to walk, there's bravery there that they must take that first step knowing they are going to fall down; but they do it. They want to learn or they want to do that, to make themselves better. They don't even realize it, but they are developing bravery at that stage. You need bravery to take on responsibilities and way back then to start hunting, especially when it came to buffalo, 'cause you could get killed. If you are a young man wanting to improve your status or to do something for your people, so as a young warrior, you take that step to go out with a war party. You need that bravery to do that, to face the enemy, to face danger. Even to pick up a Sacred Pipe, the bravery that is there there's a lot of responsibility that comes with that. It's like a mother having a child, it changes her life seriously and it complicates it, to a point where there's more responsibility, more growth, it's a good complication. She uses more of her thinking, more of her energy towards caring. But you need that bravery to take these steps. Sometimes fear is there and you have to overlook that or say I'll deal with that. Sometimes just being lazy holds people back on bravery. A long time ago, people were very active, they were moving, using energy, helping out doing things, you couldn't afford to be lazy. People would talk about that, tease you about that. They wouldn't hurt your feelings by yelling at you, so they might just tease you in a subtle way.

The bravery was the first step of virtue followed by fortitude, once you accept the responsibility. That responsibility can be just being Lakota itself: being a man or a woman, being a father or a mother, being a hunter, being a warrior, being a leader, being a Medicine Man or what they call just a common man, *ikce wicasa* . If you make a vow to Sun Dance, to *hanbleceya* for four days say, the second day, you may start to complain, it starts to get tough. You might say, "Well I'm thinking about quitting." Well you should have thought about before you made the commitment, the vow. We don't want you to quit, no matter how hard it is. We want you to go the distance, no quitting. No matter what kind of fears you have: what kind of thinking you have, go the distance. Same thing as a father, go the distance, that's your child. Work with that child. It's hard to do sometimes, in the modern day, when there's divorce, separation. But still you have a responsibility there even if you are not living with that person. So this fortitude is there, if you are in battle, don't quit half way through the battle. Go the distance, even through rough times, through a long winter or real hot summer there's no quitting, you have to move on, you have to get the job done.

Then there's generosity. You are born into this world; the old saying is, with nothing. We might go out of this world with nothing. The Great Spirit, we believe once had everything. He gave it all away: all of His power, His knowledge, His Spirit, all of these things. He became hard like a rock. But what He gave away was to make this creation, this universe. They say His breath is like the air that we breathe. What we see, His body is everything. His Spirit is in everything. The power that He has came by doing that, if you love so much, you give it all away with no fears. He became hard like a rock, but He still has the respect, the authority and the Spirits. Other religions might have angels, helpers, whatever comes to earth to help. The Spirits, they still go to Him, they still advise Him. He still has the authority, the wisdom and so we still recognize Him. So when we pray to the Sun during the Sun Dance we are worshiping *Wi* the Sun. We recognize that is an entity. In our religion, our way of life our thinking is that its coming down to sixteen major Spirits or entities that make up our universe, our world. *Tunkashila* or *Wakan Tanka* the Great Spirit is without power per se, but with all the authority and so He is on top. All these other Spirits, the helpers, there's other Spirits, we recognize that, but that's an example of generosity by the Great Spirit and Spirits sense that example.

So we as humans follow that example of generosity or we did anyhow. We give what we have. A long time ago, talking 100, 150 years ago even, we could easily give up our horses. You could even give up your teepee, the buffalo hides, all of these things, all of your possessions. You would think, I can get those back somehow and in a good way. I can go out there and make another teepee. I could go out there and somebody will give me a horse, because our people were known to be a giving people. Not a taking people, but a giving people. Sadly to say, some of those things have changed. Our thinking has changed into a more materialistic way to where there's more greed for possessions and material wealth, a lot of us think that way. I'm thinking that we justify it that that's the way we're supposed to live. We work, take our money, we buy things. Notice that a lot of the elders will get a check. They'll give their money away to their children, grandchildren and some people that need help. They're broke two days later. "Boy, can't you save money grampa or gramma?" "Uh a little bit. I bought a little bit of things but I know that somebody needs it more than me." But it's that philosophy of giving and giving everything, so a lot of our people are broke. Yeah we practice it to a certain degree, but nothing like we did a long time ago. Maybe this story addresses that and a lot of times when we see someone who's greedy or stingy or maybe they have a lot of things we mention that and they hear it. Why does that person need four cars? Can't they help out his sister or somebody that doesn't have one? It comes into play; we try to keep each other in check. Then there is a fine line between that and jealousy. Somebody might get jealous and want to destroy something. Somebody else might want to steal it, take it or they might get mad about it. But if you do it in a good way and you understand that and you learn from that, that there is a balance there that you are looking for. It needs to be talked about more, if not, the way that we are going, we'll all be looking for individual wealth and that big part of our life, of sharing and of giving, practicing this generosity and not just once or twice a year during Christmas or during a giveaway or during a ceremony or a *wopila* might be gone forever. Try to practice it more, a little bit each day and it comes back to you. That's not what you look for, but that's what happens is it comes around. People remember that. People feel good about getting something, a gift from somebody and you don't expect it back but it'll come back to you some good way.

The last virtue would be wisdom. The man is probably more known for it as a spiritual leader as a chief. We rely on these people for their leadership and their interpretation, their wisdom to make good decisions, to lead us in a good way, protect us, help us and help us to understand the unknown or the mysteries. We will never know all the mysteries, but at least to understand it in a way to deal with it, deal with death, life, sorrows. In the woman, naturally their road through being a baby, a little girl prepares them. We have ceremonies for becoming a woman. Another ceremony or a part of their life is when they're married and have children. Another big part of their life is making things, preparing things, carrying all the way up until middle age and then into being an elder. The example that they follow is *Unci Maca*, Grandmother Earth, what she does for us. This is their teacher. That her entity, the earth is a woman, takes care of us, provides for us, gives us shelter, feeds us, gives us a path to follow in life. That this is very physical. It's there and they use what they can and follow nature to make life easier but meaningful. That's important, a meaningful life and with that and with the man, that's why life was so good for us a long time ago. But you can still practice these things but it's not as much as much as people are practicing how we lived a long time ago. Those four virtues a Medicine Man could probably tell you better than me. There are some things I know just off the top of my head.

Twenty Seven - Melvin Miner and Sidney Keith
Food

I was working with the Rapid City Indian Health Advisory Board and they would have conferences and workshops and everyone had a concern over our health: physical health, emotional health, our diet, our lifestyle, our way of thinking, our spirituality, our physical well being. A lot of things have happened to our people, some brought on by others, some we bring on our self. Sidney always addressed the physical and mental well being, in relationship problems he would help people with.

I remember he was talking and he said, "You know a long time ago we had this four legged relative, *Tatanka*. We didn't have too many sicknesses. This is all new to us. Starting with the arrival of the white man, we caught a lot of diseases and the smallpox was probably the most deadly. But even before that we really knew how to take care of food; preparing food, smoking food, storing food, preserving it. One way was that we boiled our food, our meat. We would have elders, people with not to strong teeth so they couldn't eat the meat cooked up over just the fire. It was too tough. So we would boil it. Just like turnips. They would pick the turnips. They let them dry out. They would become hard like a jawbreaker, like rock candy. So they would have to soak it the night before. Then the next day, you can boil it and it would be nice and soft. A lot of this is for the children also and the elders, so they could eat meat and have that strength. But by boiling it, it also killed any bacteria or germs that might be with that meat. They have to use it right away. To let it spoil, they would be wasting meat, would be wasting a life of a buffalo. Even to have a part of that spoiled they didn't feel good about, so mainly the women took precautions to utilize everything they could as far as cooking or preserving the meat. The men would utilize whatever else there was with that buffalo and there was a lot of buffalo. There could be a lot one day, they still could go out and slaughter whatever they could handle. They would take it and if they got more than they could use, they made sure they got that to other bands, relatives of their camp. They just couldn't afford to over kill, that was a lesson"

Sidney knew a lot about food. But going back further, right around the reservation time, 1890's and early 1900's people still knew the stories, still knew the methods of collecting food. They would always offer something for that life of the buffalo, elk or deer. Give some tobacco or give a prayer or give a song and that was to ensure that somebody would gain health from that food, gain strength, so they can help their people keep on living in a good way. Then when they eat it, they have a prayer over that food again. It was a daily practice and everybody knew that that was a ritual. Today we do that but maybe it's not as much as they did it before.

Kububu Bread, Chokecherries, Wasna, Wojapi- Sidney Keith

Well that's easy to make. Anybody can make that. Just put flour and a little water in there. Just mix it up. Before they had this baking powder and stuff, they just make a grate, with flour coming out. Put that on top and then before it gets too hot you flip it over and back. Like that, put your hand on it and it'll keep rising, so you pat it, *kabubu* it. Sometimes they call it *kabubu*. Later years they had baking powder. Put a little of it in there and it raises by itself. You *kabubu* it before you put it on the stove and it raises very nice. That's why they say *kabubu* bread. That's all you do is *kabubu*. It means something you pat. But it's just as good as fried bread. It's not as greasy. Some people make real good fried bread, you know. But there's no grease in it. They use something else. Crisco, that's what they use. So you're not eating greasy bread. It's Crisco.

Ceyaka, (Wild Mint) makes a good tea. They use it in ceremonies, too. The Spirits really like it. Anything that they discovered many years ago, the Spirits really like that better. You put steak out, like we do today: and fry bread. *Papa* (dried meat) is all right and potato soup is good, they drink the soup.

That's called the *wicipan* there: *canpa icapan* (chokecherry pounder). That's what it's for, *canpa.* That's what they used to pound the cherries. Put the chokecherries in there, you pound 'em. That bag catches all that stuff. If it gets too much, why, they put it on there. They make patties and dry it, then they put it away for the winter. She usually takes a handful and three or four at a time, she keeps pounding it until its real flat. My grandmother used to, her hands would be purple after a certain time of the year (laughing) in August. Some they make the red type, when they're red, that's when they do dried meat. Some, they do it later. There is a difference depending on when you cook it, it's a little different. It has a little flavor, better. They're all the same. But the earlier one, you mix it with *papa* (dried pounded meat) to make that *wasna*. That's how they do it. But this other, this later one, is for *wojapi* (chokecherry pudding). The cherries that are really ripe, because the earlier ones, you'll have the runs (chuckling) because they're too early if you made *wojapi* out of them. Your throat is sore, that's why they call it chokecherries. So you have to wait till they're ripe, to make the *wojapi*. But the other one is good for *wasna*, because that sets, I don't know what it does, something to the *wasna*. Now they use the strainers. They usually strain it, then they put it in the *wojapi*, add flavor and make it, you know pudding.

Twenty Eight - Sidney Keith
Assimilation

Nowadays, it's different. You can't tell them little kids anything. Nowadays, you'll get a fight out of it (chuckling, but sadly). It's really different. That's why I say the social system is breaking up, to the point of extinction. Now like my brother and his kids, he has mostly boys; in my family they're all girls, except one; and he has all boys and he's got two girls. When I was their age, my uncle was like my Dad and my Aunt was like my mother; and my cousins were like my brothers and the girls were too, my cousins. And the cousin, always the cousin, even down to fourth, fifth, or first cousin, we all treated alike. Nowadays, that's not so. A couple months ago; I knew my brother had a younger girl that I haven't seen, because she's always in school. Here, all the rest of 'em knew me, but she didn't. They come around if they need some money, or something, you know, help like that. But as far as my wife goes, they don't call her Aunt, they call her Shirley. You see, right there, it's different. And this one, little one, they said, "Do you know him?" You know, one time I was sitting with her mother when she came in. "Who is that?" I said. She said, "That's your niece." I said, "*Hwo?*" (Is that so?) "That's Raymond's girl." So, she shook my hand, but she looked at me kind of funny (chuckling). She doesn't believe it. She probably doesn't believe her uncle's got to be so old. So, it's really no good.

And my mother, she still has a *sic'esi*, you know, a cousin; and they're still goin' at it like the old days. Still close and their children are *takoja*. She doesn't know them, but their kids will come and say, "Grandmother" and she'll ask them to identify, who's their dad, who's their mother; and she'll say:" Oh, oh, sit down. There's some *wotapi* (food) here." So she still retains that because of her age. But nowadays that's going out of style, really.

It's like, when was it, the 1930's around there, when they started giving out nursing bottles, instead of women nursing. When P.H.S. (Public Health Service) came to the rest of them and started this bottle feeding business. So nowadays, kids think that's funny, when you say you want to nurse it. My mother told a woman to nurse her baby, "Are you kidding?" she replied. (Laughing)

I think I nursed 'til I was two years old. Until you know you don't have to. It reminds me, when I was a little boy, soon as I could remember, I could still see boys my age nursing. Big shoes on, laying there, you know, they were just doing something, lying under here (gesturing under arm), nursing while she was trying to do something, you know (chuckling). It's really funny, but that's the way it used to be. That's the way they grew up to be strong. They eat, they nurse, a mother's milk is the best thing there is. Now, it's the bottle. You don't know if it's cow's milk or what.

It's assimilation. Because when I go around lecturing, that's the first thing I tell them. That assimilation is a bad word and it's a devilish thing, but it's gotta be. And I believe that it's because over the years I've been an Indian, a traditional man, all my life. My kids were well trained, up to a point and that means when I moved into town and then they started changing. These kids don't want the old ways. They want loud music. They want to watch TV. Now the teenagers, they want to just listen to the rock type music, but that's okay. As long as they still do their Indian dance, too. They do. Three of my girls have Sun Danced and they know how to dance, pretty fancy Pow Wow dancing. They know a few words of Indian, so I'm doing good, as far as I'm concerned. I told 'em that: You learn yours, too and you learn the White Man's and you're gonna make it. You've got good sense and you can do both. Because you can't be a brown-skinned White Man. You can't be a red 'Apple', either. So you'll have to do both to succeed. Our boy is doing that, he's got a car, but he's always got an eagle feather inside. Not just because everybody else has got one, he has a purpose. He knows quite a lot about the culture. So this next year, he's going to graduate, so that's a really good accomplishment, for my family. He will succeed, because he knows both cultures. If he fails, he can go back the other way, jump back in like that. But what the B.I.A. is doing is, "Forget your Culture. Forget your language. Forget all that stuff. Be a White Man."

It's getting worse. A lot of times we ask to use the gymnasium. Being the President of the Sioux Nation Arts Council, we support drama, the theatre and sometimes we like to bring in movies like Enter the Dragon is a show, you know. And they say okay. But later I might say, "We'd like to use your gym." They say, "For what?" I say, "A Pow Wow." They say, "No. (Chuckling) No way." I asked them why. They said, "Oh, you'll break everything." And then the White Men come and say, "Can we use your gym for a dance?" "Sure." Well, they break up more things than Pow Wows do, you know. They drink. At Pow Wows you're not supposed to drink and if they do, why they'll throw you out. So it's hard, because they, you don't see it, but you feel it. They don't want you to do that.

Like the Sun Dance. Nobody supports that, **nobody**. People coming in support that, other tribes. We tried it, but it didn't work. (Laughing) We wrote a letter and we took it to the local men. One guy gave us a quart of oil, on the grass. (Laughing) That was the tailgate of that soliciting. And stuff like that, you know.

My job was to save the culture. That's all I've been trying to do. Talking like this. Painting like this (indicating the huge murals which so beautifully adorn the Cultural Center). But it's always a losing battle. I told 'em, "I'll never give up, as long as two Indians are left, we'll still be talking."

Assimilation is the worst thing that can happen. About twenty or thirty years ago, when I was at school at the Old Agency, they were pushing that Traditional Culture. They'd say, "How about you kids get a drum and everybody sing. Let's start a dance." So they did and all the teachers come and they dance around, you know. They thought that was fun. So the kids never had that problem in school. Everybody went to school, eight in the morning, nine in the morning. Nowadays, they don't do that. So, what? They think they are going to run this White society way and learn that? That's all they want you to do anyway: Think White. You've gotta eat and sleep White. So that's when they foul up, because they can't cope. They say, "No. I'm an Indian." But who's he gonna tell? Who is he gonna tell that he's an Indian? They can't do it that way, no.

In those days when I went to school, I couldn't talk English anyway. So I think it was good that they didn't talk Indian in school at that time. After I got up to the fourth grade, I think, I started to learn how to talk English pretty good, especially at school. So beyond that, I think maybe it was good that we weren't able to talk a lot. But other places, I went to school in

Phoenix, Arizona, they were the opposite. They were pretty mean about speaking, over there. The Navajo's couldn't talk their language and they soaped their mouth if they do, or whipped them. That was a little different. I don't know if there was any difference there, but it was certainly a mean way to do it. The approach was different.

The old Agency was a B.I.A. school, but I think those people working there were a little more concerned for the students and they didn't have that racial attitude, like now. And that's a lot different, there. That's another thing that I used to talk about in education. Before the school starts I'll stand at that bridge and stop everybody and say, "Are you a teacher?" They say, "Yes, I'm a teacher." "Well, I want to ask you a few questions. Do you know anything about Sioux Indians?" She'll say, "No." "Do you know the history of Indians, the Sioux?" "No." "Do you like Indians?" "No." "No? Well then you've got no business there." Or I would say, "Are you interested in Indians?" "Yes." "Do you want to learn about Indians?" "Yes." "And do you know the culture? Do you know the history of the Sioux?" They say, "Yes." "Okay, we want you."

I think that's the way they should do, instead of letting people come in from places where they don't know nothing about the Sioux. They think they know about Indians, but they're different. You know there's a lot of difference between each tribe, especially here in South Dakota. I think we're the main tribe; the Sioux. The Plains Indian is the Sioux. We carried a lot of weight, in the 18th century we did, we carried a lot of weight. All the other tribes didn't know how to do this and do that, we had to be the leaders. So I think that's the way that we should get our teachers; I think they gotta be qualified.

They're usually qualified, these doctors that come in, too. (Mr. Keith was employed at the Public Health Service Hospital in Eagle Butte.) I tell them about how the Indians feel. They use their language, the old people. If they're talking in Indian, they're not talking about you. If they're talking and laughing, they're not laughing at you. They've got a funny language, when they talk, they laugh at each other; they make fun of each other and they laugh at it. Those things, if you understand that, you're gonna get along with the Indians. If you go in there with a chip on your shoulder, it's not gonna work. They'll run you out of there." And it works. The doctor said, "It's a good thing you told me." Those are the ones that usually stay all the way through. They have to stay two years. Well, they stay two years, some of them; so that's not really too bad. The ones that don't want to, just come for money, it's different. Actually, they want to step on everybody. Some are too young and they just come to have a real good time, there's that type too.

You've got to look at the Indian too, you've got to look at that, see how they're thinking, see how they do things. The one's, you know like Jim Gillihan. He's really good. He used to be at Pierre. He was President of Cultural Preservation. He was really good there. He was always talking to the Indians, learning stuff like that. Pretty soon he had his own pipe and he prayed and he finally caught on, you know; and he was thinking like an Indian, so that's why. The last time I seen him was in an airport and he came over. All these White people standing, I was the only Indian standing there. He seen me and he come over and shook hands with me. He said, "I've seen you someplace." "Ya," I said. "Ya, we sweated together." I told him my name and he said, "Ya, I know you." So people like that, they mean it. They don't have that racial attitude.

Those are the good people; those are the ones that succeed, the way we do things, they're gonna succeed that way. So I think they took a lung out, but they prayed for him and he prayed with his pipe, that he wasn't gonna die, he was gonna be successful, he did. Last time I seen, that time I saw him, he was just all bones and they were pushing him around in a wheelchair, but again he come up, they pushed him over and he shook hands again. The next time I saw him, he was down here. I shook hands with him again; he was walking, looked real good. He was prayed for and the religion helped him through a terrible ordeal. He said, "*Woicupo!*" (I have been helped!). So it takes the good people with the right mind, to fully understand the Indian and Indians will always like you. But somebody like Janklo (Attorney General of South Dakota, then currently running for the office of Governor) on the other hand, nobody likes him, Indians you know. His attitude is mostly... (laughing).

Twenty Nine - Sidney Keith
Mitakuye Oyasin

We are all created equal, we are two legged animals too. History tells us that maybe we were a baboon one time or something. So therefore, the human is not supposed to be above the animals. We can be smart, but only at certain things. We can be smart as hell and we are smarter than the animals. They can't talk, unless they're Spirits, but they talk to each other. So the four major races are supposed to be like that. But now we're smarter than the animals! We dug up their habitat. Plow it up! Blow it up! Dig it out! Just raise heck with the environment! It affects the whole animal world; eagles included, even man, especially the Indians, because this used to be our land, so it hurts the Indians worst.

But it's only gonna go up so far, then it's gonna come down to go back where it was in the beginning. They are going to show us a vision from the East and the Indian is gonna see it first. At the end of the world they are going to see this Pipe, see how powerful it is. Up in Heaven, the Pipe is gonna be up there, that Calf Pipe Woman's gonna be there and gonna show you that power. She's gonna show it to you up there in Heaven. It could be understood that way. You know what they're doing now? The Medicine Man is praying, when he faces east, "We want to see that vision right now." Because of everything that is going wrong for the Indians, their land being taken away, everything. They want that world to come back, if this is how it's gonna be, they're gonna show us that the world is gonna end in the next decade. We want to see it now, so that we can be prepared to go up there, rather than suffer down here. That's what they're doing. That's what they're praying. They want to see that vision. In other words, they want to end the world. That's what's gonna end one day.

It's not the end of the world itself, but something is gonna happen to the world, so they'll be nothing living on the earth. It will be all Spirits going someplace. But the world will be continued, this moon, the sun will be sitting there, everything will keep going round and round, but everything on the earth, it's gonna be gone. Only the Great Spirit is gonna be there. Maybe later on it will start all over again. That's why they say, "Next time I'm gonna be something else, when I come back" This ties into everything, way up there in the galaxy, in the stars, it all ties in together.

Epilogue

I never got to meet Sidney Keith. He passed away at the age of 77 years in Rapid City, South Dakota on June 14, 1997. As a man he wore many hats; Husband, Father, Grandfather. He was a talented artist, with many paintings, political cartoons, Christmas cards and murals. He was a spiritual leader who kept his native culture from disappearing. He worked to preserve the Lakota language and authored his own dictionary. He rallied to preserve the Black Hills and worked to return Paha Sapa to its rightful owners as described in the Fort Laramie Treaty of 1868.

Melvin Vincent Miner Jr. was born on August 4, 1956 in Igloo, South Dakota. I truly dread remembering this but on December 15, 2010 I got a phone call from a mutual friend. It's a cliché but I had to sit down when I got the news. Melvin had died that morning from what we found out later was a massive heart attack. I had talked to him just two days before and he seemed fine. He wasn't feeling well that morning and was on his way to the hospital when he left us and went to the Spirit World.

There is more to this story than what can fit in this book. Consider this to be part one of a story about the lives of two people that deeply touched everyone they encountered. I have kept my promise to Melvin to finish this book. I humbly offer this book to the world and hope to touch even more lives with the stories of Sidney Keith and Melvin Miner.

Chapter Notes
Chapter One

The words of Sidney Keith in Chapter One and in subsequent chapters comes from four documents. The South Dakota Oral History Center at the University of South Dakota houses thousands of documents consisting of interviews of residents of South Dakota. The interviews used were as follows:

An Interview with Sidney Keith, Green Grass, South Dakota, May 12, 1976 John S. Painter, Interviewer American Indian History Project, Northern State College, Aberdeen South Dakota AIRP 1711 – AIH 76.11

An Interview with Sidney Keith, Green Grass, South Dakota May 14, 1976. John S. Painter, Bruce Pudwell, Linda Jo Matz, Interviewers. AIRP 1712. AIH 76.12

An Interview with Sidney Keith, Eagle Butte, South Dakota. May 21, 1976. John S. Painter, Interviewer. AIRP 1715 AIH 76.15

Transcript of an interview with Mr. Sidney Keith, Eagle Butte, Cheyenne River Sioux Reservation, South Dakota. Recorded by Michael Cowdrey, Curator. W.H. Museum, Vermillion, South Dakota,

September 30, 1978. SDOHP 1974, AIRP 523.

Used with permission of The Oral History Center University of South Dakota.

The name of the Medicine Man who got Sidney on the path was omitted from the original interview. I could not verify the name so it stands as omitted.

Chapter Two

The words of Melvin Miner are from cassette tapes provided by Melvin Miner in November of 2009 for this book. The tapes were transcribed by myself and follow up questions were asked by phone and in person.

Chapter Three

Sidney talks about the origin of the Sun Dance, the Sacred Pipe and what they mean to the Lakota people. He briefly talks about the family history of the Pipe keepers. The Sacred Pipe is further discussed later in the text.

Chapter Four

I have an interview from Joe Rockboy where he states his unconditional belief in using peyote (AIRP 889). When I told Melvin this he was truly surprised. Maybe Joe just didn't want Melvin to go to the Peyote Ceremony.

Chapter Five

Sidney talks about Frank Fools Crow, beloved Spiritual Leader of the Lakota. For further information about Frank Fools Crow I would recommend the books authored by Thomas E. Mails.

Chapter Six

Melvin told the tale of the magpies on his roof.

Sidney included the following note about magpies in his English to Lakota Dictionary.

The *unkce kihaka* (magpie) is considered by the Lakota's to be a dirty bird because his nest is very simple and badly constructed and is always full of bird manure. Also, whenever some one kills an animal and brings it in at night, the magpie will sit atop the tipi and jabber until shooed away. When somebody shows up they have to share a piece of meat.

Orthography English to Lakota Dictionary by S. Keith. Copies of the dictionary are very hard to find. Hopefully the dictionary will be back in print soon.

Chapter Seven

I combined several parts from the interviews to create the story of the pipestone and the tools and plants that are part of the use of the pipe.

Chapter Eight

Melvin created the Black Hills Pow Wow with the help of many. Melvin was honored post humously at the 25th anniversary of the Pow Wow in October of 2011.

Chapter Nine

Sidney talks about not being a Medicine Man at this point in his life in 1976. He organized the International Sun Dance at Green Grass, South Dakota in 1971. This was the first Sun Dance to be held in the open on the Cheyenne River Reservation in many years. Up until the passage of the American Indian Religious Freedom Act in 1978 the open practice of traditional ceremonies was illegal.

Chapter Ten

Melvin shares the story of his first Sun Dance.

Chapter Eleven

Sidney shares the journey of getting more power and more help from the Spirits on his path to becoming a Medicine Man.

Chapter Twelve

Melvin shares some of his memories of being around his father-in-law and mother-in-law.

Chapter Thirteen

Sidney talks about his family history of Medicine Men. He refers to his Grandfather Ray Eagle Chaser. Other sources use the name Eagle Chasing. This is not an error but rather the fluidity of the Lakota language. I am not an expert or even fluent in the language but humbly wish to point out this matter.

Chapter Fourteen

Source Big Foot Ride: The Rapid City Journal-Carson Walker, The Associated Press-Posted: Sunday, December 14, 2008 11:00 pm

Chapter Fifteen

Sidney shares insights and stories about the sacred clown known as the Heyoka.

Chapter Sixteen

Melvin first mentions hmunga when he is at college. Sidney expands on the subject in greater depth. I haven't seen this practice mentioned anywhere else in such depth.

Chapter Seventeen

A great story about what can be done when people work together with each other and the Spirits. The inipi is still being used by a great many people in Rapid City.

Chapter Eighteen

Melvin said the following about curing the spiritual leader.

"I don't know how we could write this up. I'd have to give the persons name, anyhow I don't know how were going to tell this story. I think it's important because it does have a lot of meaning to it, actually medicine men curing or helping other medicine men so we'll keep it in there. We'll see how it is written up. The Medicine Man is still alive so I don't want him to get mad at me or something."

I included the story with great respect towards the afflicted person and Melvin. I do not know the identity of the person mentioned. I felt it was an important story that illustrates the give and take present in the spiritual world.

Also in that vein concerning the Wandering Spaniard Spirit, Melvin later told me off the tape the reason the Spirit was wearing out his welcome. The Spirit would pull the covers off the wife at night, just her. So that Spirit was a Horny Spirit and that's why the family wanted him to leave. All respect to the Spirit mentioned.

Chapter Nineteen

In the interviews, the subject of a vision that Martin High Bear must have shared in a ceremony came up several times. I have asked myself why the interviewers didn't ask Mr. High Bear themselves for the "English" translation. Apparently Martin High Bear was not available to answer the questions that the interviewers had. I consulted a good friend who is an expert in matters of the Spirit world and of tact. He said to use my intuition. I searched Martin High Bear on the internet and found an interview with Mr. High Bear. He gave me my answer, so with all due respect to Martin High Bear and Sidney Keith; here is what Sidney had to say about Martin's vision.

Chapter Twenty

I hesitated to include this first story. In another day and another time there would be no problem describing what happened. In our current politically correct and cloistered society all I can say is this. It was a hard thing to do, and Melvin and Sidney handled the situation with dignity and respect for the dog.

Chapter Twenty One

Once again I hesitated to include the 50per cent cure, so did Melvin. I included the story to illustrate that the Spirits are serious business and any ceremony should be approached with respect.

Chapter Twenty Two

Melvin talks about the Black Hills Treaty. Sidney worked very hard over the years to keep the treaty in the minds of the people. There have been volumes written on the subject that the interested reader can access.

Chapter Twenty Three

I never had the privilege of meeting Sidney Keith face to face. I included the Whoopee Cushion and Iktomi stories to illustrate the sense of humor present in the Lakota culture. Whenever I spend time with my Lakota friends my face and ribs hurt from laughing so much. Some might consider the story risqué, I consider the story to be just what it is, a funny story.

Chapter Twenty Four

Melvin talks eloquently about the spiritual aspects of the Lakota.

Chapter Twenty Five

Melvin talks about Pipe protocol.

Chapter Twenty Six

Melvin talks about history and virtues.

Chapter Twenty Seven

The kububu bread story was in one of the interviews. I really could not believe the interviewers wanted to know so much about this. It fits in this section just fine. The chokecherry pounder referred to is from an interview where Sidney walked around a collection of traditional tools, artifacts and pictures and commented on them.

Chapter Twenty Eight

This is a great discourse by Sidney on the values and trials of the then current generation that applies to today as well. The story ends with Sidney talking (or gesturing) about Bill Janklow who passed away while this book was in its final stages of completion. Like my own Grandmother said, if you can't say something nice about someone, don't say anything at all.

Chapter Twenty Nine

Is it a message of hope? Is it a warning? I will let the reader decide.

Glossary

Lakota words and phrases were checked against the text provided in the Oral History Interviews. The words were also checked against the Lakota- English Dictionary compiled by Rev. Eugene Buechel. Also used was the Orthography English to Lakota Dictionary by Sidney Keith. Merle Whistler also provided much needed advice and support.

akicaska- to sew or baste on
azillia (azilya) - to smudge
canhlogan- hollow stalks, weeds
canka hohwa- grass with a hole in it
cannumpa- a pipe
cannumpa icasloke- pipe, to clean it
cannumpa iyuhaha izitka - pipe ornamented to smoke
cannumpa sa- red pipe
cannumpa sapa- black pipe
Cannumpa Wakan- sacred blessed pipe
cansasa- red willow bark for smoking
cantojuha- heart, container
catkaata (catkayatanhan) - on the left
cekpa ognake- umbilical cord, bag to put it in
ceyaka -wild mint
chungliska- cigarettes

dako wakan- that that is holy; that which has a spirit.
gicicetu -to stumble or misstep
hanbleceya- vision quest; crying for a vision
He Sapa-the Black Hills
heyoka- a person who because of their vision is a clown
hmunga- to cause sickness; to cause kindly enchantment; to bewitch; (to send a sharp missile into the body of another, with the aid of supernatural power).
honeh choon-they did
hunkapi- making of relatives ceremony
hununpa- two leggeds; a human
hwo- Is that so?
ikce wicasa- a common man,
iho-behold, listen, be it so
iktomi- a spider; a creature of folklore
inikagapi wokeya- a sweatlodge
inipi- a steaming, sweating
inyan sa- red stone
intercessors- those who work for the Medicine Man at a Sun Dance
interpretate- to examine and explain a dream or vision
itokagata- the south direction
kola- friend
lowanpi-singing ceremony
magajukte (magajukiya) - to cause to rain

mastinca pute -rabbits lip
miniapapson-water word
miyoglasin- a mirror, looking glass
nagi- the soul, spirit. the shadow of anything
ojuha- beaded or quilled
onjinjintka- rose hips
opagi- offer of tobacco to a Medicine Man
owinja paskiskapi- quilted
pangi- wild beets
parfleche-a hard dried animal hide usually made into bags or shields
paskiska- put together
peji to swuwela- grass, blue, soft
peji to waste- grass, blue, good
pilama- thank you
sic'esi- a cousin
sota- smoke
takoja-children
taleja- bladder
tatanka-buffalo
tahinspa- needle
t' elanuwe- horned toad
tinpsila -prairie turnips
timahel- inside the house, within
tiospaye- extended family
tiwahay- family
Tunkashila (Tunkasila) - the Supreme Being, a grandfather, my grandfather

Unci Maca- Grandmother Earth
unkce kihaka- magpie
wablenica- orphan
wagmuha- scrotum – used to make a rattle
wahununpa- the Spirit that walks
wahutopa- the four leggeds
wahupakoza- legs, swinging back and forth, birds
wakan- sacred, consecrated
wakiyans- the thunder beings
wanagi (nagi) - the soul when separated from the body; a ghost, the Spirits of the departed; a shadow
wanagi peji hota- spirit, grass, grey
Wanbli Gleska- the spotted eagle; the epitome of powers of the north
wase- red earth, vermillion
wasicun- a white man
wasposli patapi- face covering embroidered
wasna-spirit food
waste lo- good, with emphasis
wazilya- incense
waziyata- the north direction
wi- the Lakota word for sun
Wicahpi Oyate-the Star People
wiyohiyanpata- the east direction
wiyohpeyata- the west direction
woken wokazeze- baby cradle

woicupo- I have been helped
wopila- thanks; a thank you gifting ceremony
wotapi- food
wowahwa- peace
yuwipi- to tie; ceremony where the Medicine Man is tied

A Common Man

www.ingramcontent.com/pod-product-compliance
Lightning Source LLC
Chambersburg PA
CBHW032033150426
43194CB00006B/257